# EAT, FUCK, (write about) MURDER

## BY GINA TRON

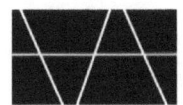

***Eat, Fuck, (write about) Murder*** ©**2023** by **Gina Tron**. Published in the United States by V.A. Press. Not one part of this work may be reproduced without expressed written consent from the author. For more information, please write V.A. Press, 643 South 2nd Street, Milwaukee, WI 53204

**Cover art by Ryan Cayia**

**ISBN:** 978-1-952055-52-2

In *Eat, Pray, Love,* the protagonist resolves her divorce by seeing the world. Through her travels, she finds purpose, meaning, and finally, love again. The following is a much bleaker version of that story. In the midst of breakups with a serious boyfriend and a literary agent, I do some traveling and some eating, and I write about murder, but — spoiler — I do not fall in love with someone new in this story. The main similarity between this book and *Eat, Pray, Love* is that yes, this is just yet another vapid white American woman's travel story. While the first story is one of self-actualization, mine details a continuing journey of running away from myself. At this time in my existence, I was looking for some *life* after part of my body had been murdered to avoid the whole from dying of cancer, as well as years lost to a relationship that was dead on arrival.

Dedicated to my husband, Ryan Cayia, the person whose Big Dipper markings match up with mine. Thank you for loving me as deeply as you do and for turning every moment of mundanity into magic.

# Prologue

Unlike Elizabeth Gilbert, I didn't go to the romantic settings of Naples, Rome, and then Bali for a spiritual journey and fantastic conclusion. I ventured to Sicily's largest city and the epicenter of carbombings and mafia death in the 90s, Palermo. How fitting for a person whose job is to write about murder all day. I had been working as a contractor for Oxygen since 2017, halfway through grad school and halfway through multiple surgeries for breast cancer.

In my cover letter for the job, I wrote about getting raped and about writing a death threat in high school. It was the most candid I'd ever been in a cover letter; I wanted to prove that I was versatile, that I had been at different angles of the justice system to some extent, that I'm both a criminal and a victim, just like everyone else in life. *I'm in the gray area and I know it; most people think of the world as black and white, and I do not. Hire me!* I'd covered a bunch of murder stuff already too, so that helped.

It was the autumn of 2018. I was now in the best job of my life, even though I wasn't technically even employed by them. I was a remote contractor working full time hours, who could work from home, a cafe, a bar, parking lot, a pool, a gas station. Sure, I didn't get benefits, but the pay was good for a writer.

I could live anywhere as long as there was wifi. So, why would I stay in Vermont post-breakup while autumn was deepening? I would undoubtedly just fall into deep depression as my coupled-up friends hibernated and single friends made haste to cuff up for winter. I'd only drink and eat all day then go to bed at 9 pm, possibly abusing substances I shouldn't, as the days grew colder, darker, lonelier, more desperate. No thanks. Plus, I would have ended up fucking people I shouldn't, or putting drama where I shouldn't. Vermont is too small to do that without major consequences.

Sony Pictures describes the movie *Eat Pray Love* as follows: "Liz Gilbert (Roberts) had everything a modern woman is supposed to dream of having - a husband, a house, a successful career - yet like so many others, she found herself lost, confused, and searching for what she really wanted in life. Newly divorced and at a crossroads, Gilbert steps out of her comfort zone, risking everything to change her life, embarking on a journey around the world that becomes a quest for self-discovery."

I didn't have everything a modern woman is supposed to dream of having to begin with. I'm a fucking millennial with dead non-rich parents. You really thought I would have a house by now? And while the following is a breakup story, I didn't get divorced. Just left a boyfriend who was hesitating to propose to me. Instead of marriage, I had cancer. And I lost both parents to it before ever even discussing getting engaged with any dude.

Most of my life was lived by the mantra "I would rather never get married than marry the wrong person," but I was starting to feel a different kind of cancer growing in me: the increasingly painful feeling that I'd missed out.

Getting married. Having a partner. Having a normal life. Having the kind of life stupid movies, books, and friends all tell me I'm supposed to want. The things they push me to think about when I tell them about writing successes. They don't want to hear about literary accolades. They want to hear about whose dick I'm playing with. They are hoping that I'll marry one of those dicks. They look at me with pity because I haven't yet.

Because then I can become normal. Then I can have a non-threatening life.

# Kyle

I wasn't touching *any* dicks while I was still with Kyle. Not even his. Even though I seemed to have a nice enough life from the outside, it felt incredibly alone.

While late 2016 was all about getting my tits chopped off, 2017 was all about getting new ones plastered on, then removed after complications, then crammed on again, then going under the knife one final time to get lipo in an effort to make my new flesh lumps look more human. But the two surgical lines across my chest made me feel like more of a deranged coin bank than a human. I remember, before that initial dreaded surgery - the big one, expressing my sex concerns to Kyle.

"What if you won't want to fuck me anymore?" I whimpered with tears in my eyes, my legs sprawled over his on our L-shaped couch surrounded by warm lamps and wood panel windows. I remembered sitting on his face on the very same couch just weeks earlier, while the looming threat of cancer surgery seemed in the future, not the now.

"Of course I'll want to fuck you Gina. I love you. I'll still be attracted to you if you're just a head or a brain in a jar."

The anxiety erupting within me instantly retreated back into my throat with this sweet sentiment. He even bought velcro restraints for our bed for when I recovered from the surgery, hinting that we would be having all sorts of fun once I healed.

"But I'm not going to have tits anymore," I cried, a tear running down my left cheek. "I'm not going to really feel like a woman anymore."

"I don't care if you are titless," he said. "You're so sexy, I'm course I'm going to fuck you."

*Of course.*

I didn't know if he knew though, just how unsexy cancer could be. I did. I tried to dump him when I found out I had cancer. I tried to give him the out. I didn't want him to resent me the way I resented my sick mother as a pre-teen, or resent me how my father resented me for looking like my mother following her death. Kyle said he could handle it.

Spoiler: he could not. To his credit, I'm sure he thought he could. Nobody realizes the depths of such things until they're wading in them. To his credit again, he did quite well for a while.

Cut scene to one of the last times we had sex. It was October of 2016 and I still had surgical drains coming out of my sides, which he helped me clean every day. Or, as the doctor called it, milked them. Trying to keep up a positive outlook I'd make sexual jokes with Kyle as he pushed the fluids out of the tubes attached to my body.

"Drain play, baby," I'd say, sitting on the closed lid of the toilet in our cozy bathroom, staring ahead at the shower curtain's green and white stripes.

"Stop it, Gina." He'd smile as he was bent down on one knee in front of me, milking dark red bodily fluid out of me.

A few minutes later, I'd reach for him in our bed. We'd start to have sex but the drains would get tangled. I'd reach for him night after night but he wouldn't respond. My mind kept rewinding the bittersweet honeymoon stage of our relationship just months earlier.

We had sex on a bunk bed near Cape Cod, where his family had a vacation home. They were all there, so we had to be quiet. He told me he loved me during one of those restrained sex sessions. It was one of those moments I'd felt a build up to, like a volcano, so when he told me what I knew he felt, my heart erupted lava I knew I could never get back in. Now it was old lava, dried up, crusty and black.

We had only been dating for a few weeks, but it all moved fast. At some point he asked me my ring size and told me he wanted to marry me. This was before surgery but after I found out I had cancer, about one month in of dating. When we went ring shopping, my plastic surgeon was so excited for me.

"Wow, by the end of this, you'll have brand new tits and you'll be married," she said, reeking sweetly of Dior, her large eyes surrounded by mascara and black ink.

Oh boy, what else could a woman want? A dick and tits. Body parts. Sexualized body parts; that's all there is to life, one would think.

Cut scene to 2018 and I'm just basically begging for Kyle to fuck me again. Or, ya know, just have a real talk with me, or a kiss, one I didn't pressure him into. It was like we were roommates. But hell, I was much closer to all my ex-roommates than this. Even the roomies I wasn't friends with had deep conversations that felt like we were in the same room together at least once a week. It's like there was a pane of glass between me and Kyle. We could see each other, but didn't touch. There was some weird glare too. I couldn't tell what light source it was coming from, but I couldn't fully see him, or me.

Cut scene to us in Sofia, Bulgaria during the summer of 2018. We were on a trip for my friend Nathalie's wedding. As we drunkenly exited the reception early, her stepmom winked and told us, "I know what you two are up to."

No, no you don't, I wanted to tell her. We are just going to go back to our hotel room, which for 100 bucks is the equivalent of a room that would be like 700 in the states, and go to sleep, or fight. We fought, one of our worst, in that beautiful, spacious room. Then we slept. I wished I could have dreamt of that pane of glass removed between us, but I probably just dreamt of the sad reality. He had told me we would finally have sex on this trip, because we'd have more time and less distractions. Instead, he found more distractions.

Cut scene to us in Ireland, then Scotland a few days later, countries he'd wanted to visit since we'd be in Europe. I'd lay in the bed and watch television while he sat on a chair in the other room looking at Reddit. In Ireland we were enveloped by a sunlit room where at one point we saw a rainbow. In Scotland we were surrounded by a stone wall and a warm television set that revealed no murders on the news, only car crashes. I tried to initiate making out and he rejected me. I had friends in Edinburgh whom we hung out with briefly, but Kyle said he'd rather just hang with me. Except we weren't actually hanging. We were both just staring at electronic panes of glass while sitting in separate rooms, occasionally grunting at one another. The only thing he was interested in doing *with* me was eating: the haggis in Scotland and curry in Ireland were satisfying, at least.

I knew deep down we would never, ever, get engaged. The first engagement date he gave me was early 2017, just a few months after he brought up the topic. Then it was simply *soon.* Next, it was after I got my master's degree because he said he wanted me to have only the wedding and work to focus on. After I graduated in May of 2018, he said didn't have the money, even though he had just spent about $14,000 on guns. Kyle, who is liberal, bought them right after Parkland, telling me they were a great investment. I was repulsed by this reaction to such a tragedy, yet I stayed with him, which is even more repulsive on my part.

Cut scene to our birthday week, 2018, September on the edge of October. He wanted to be left alone to play *World of Warcraft* for his birthday. I got him a cake and lit the candles and brought it in while he played. He ate a slice by the warm glow of his beloved computer and I ate a slice in the living room, illuminated by the warmth of television as reality show actors bickered over the concept of betrayal. For my birthday, just a few days later, I wanted to do something together. I opted for a trip up to Montreal, where I had gone to college. We could go out to eat, definitely poutine, and maybe some drinks in the city, maybe meet up with some old friends of mine.

In the end, we didn't go anywhere, because we broke up just days before our planned excursion, onsetting a depression that surpassed even my 2016 birthday, which was spent in a hospital bed recovering from that damned double mastectomy. There was something so bitter about waking up on my birthday, the day my dead mom gave birth to me before later dying of cancer, to have to recover from cancer myself. It's just a fucking day, I guess. The best present that day was waking to the news that it was only stage one. And barely that. It hadn't spread at all.

As for the physical aspect, it was a day of immense pain, but not as painful as I expected. Not sharp like a papercut, just dull, constant, and ultimately, draining. For most of that birthday, I was immobile in a hospital gown, glaring down at all the tubes coming out of me and my suddenly super-flat chest. There were weird throbbing feelings from my body and I kept wondering why I hadn't had to pee yet, not realizing there was a catheter in me sucking it out as I struggled past the fentanyl, and whatever else, haze.

At least in that hospital bed, I was waking up to see my then-loving and supportive boyfriend who'd vowed to take care of me for the rest of my life. What a soothing thought it was. Furthermore, all the people in my life who never seemed satisfied by any achievement that I was actually proud of — writing accolades mostly — seemed suddenly puffed up with pride over the fact that I was able to rake in some man.

Any man.

I pulled up to a big Airbnb in the middle of Vermont with my Blenheim Cavalier King Charles Spaniel named Amelia in the passenger seat, the waves in her ears flowing from the slightly heated air puffing out the vents. The lake pictured in the ad was indeed across the street from the home, but the street itself was busy and loud.

I booked a two-night stay, unprepared to see anyone face-to-face yet. Still crying too much. A lakeside stint would give me time to calm down a bit. I uncorked a bottle of wine and began sobbing over *not* being able to rake in the right man, the achievement that was supposed to be the most important of all, one I never admitted meant anything to me, but secretly wanted. I just cried and cried like I was trapped in a whirlpool. I kept looking at my phone, hoping that Kyle would text me that he wanted to be with me still, that he'd made a mistake, but he didn't text at all. He was probably just in front of his computer. Trucks rumbled along the busy yet isolated road just feet from where I was sitting. I thought about how lonely it sounded, the men in trucks listening to the radio while the cold settled into their feet.

I drank until I mustered the courage to call a friend, the only person at this point I'd informed of the breakup. She reassured me I'd tried my best.

"I could have been better though," I said. "Maybe I didn't treat him right. Maybe in the beginning, I know in the beginning I lashed out at him."

"But you, you've told me this before and you apologized for it and went to therapy."

Through tears, I said, "He said I isolated him from his friends. I always told him to hang out with his friends. He was the one who never wanted to leave the house. I was cool with him being close with Dana. I told him to hang out with her still. But after that one fight, he just acted like I was just crazy about all women. I wasn't. I was mad he lied in that one specific instance.

But who cares, I shouldn't have even gotten upset with him about that."

In *Eat Pray Love*, Gilbert yells at a new man for trying to love her. He didn't even do anything wrong; he was just trying to love her. And he forgave her for yelling at him because he got it. I didn't yell but I said a few shitty things after I caught him in a lie a few months into our relationship. It basically died then. We lived in ghost land for the rest of our time together, both of us in purgatory. I was not forgiven for my sins. I instead became an unforgivable human and I'm sure he was in his own state of internal torture.

If there's one thing I do when I'm distraught, it's shower, again and again. Like a woman after she gets raped in a movie, I just want to forward time.

I stood in the Airbnb shower obsessively reliving the moment when I hurt Kyle, that one fight in which the way he thought about me changed. I could see it clearly. Us on Kyle's queen bed. I caught him in a lie about a coworker. It was a stupid lie and I didn't have to overreact.

If only I could have just calmed myself and not done that. If only I could have taken a breath. Instead, I told him, "Yeah, well I still think about how great others were at fucking me too! Just like she gave the best handjobs, some did other things better to me than you do."

It was childish, and honestly wasn't even true. Claws just came out of my hand and that's what I spit out. A mouthful I immediately regretted. I remembered Kyle running into the bathroom and crying in the shower. I remembered him never trusting me again. If only I could have not said that. Maybe we'd be married now and in our own house, I thought, while holding a white chunk of soap in my hand. It was soft and hard at the same time. I was blubbering like a baby, my cheeks like rubbery kites in the wind. After standing in that shower for what felt like hours, I got out and toweled off and stared into the mirror. I looked at my little travel bag, blue with pink flamingos on the kitchen sink. The head of my pill bottle, antidepressants, peeked out.

"I'm done taking those," I mumbled. All they seemed to do was make me gain weight during a time I already felt like I had no control over my body. They didn't help me and Kyle get along. They didn't help me feel less lonely.

I wiped a stripe through the steam that had settled on the mirror.

I could see a buildup of acne on my lower left jaw line. *You have to make sure you don't sleep on your side.* I had been doing this, along with lotions and creams and dozens of pieces of well-meaning advice, though I'm not sure it made any difference. Rage boiled like the zits boiled in my cheeks as my mind wandered down the pathway of cancer aftermath. It's so frustrating; feeling like there's a mountainous range appearing without your consent on your once-smooth cheeks. My adult acne had subsided when I went back on hormonal birth control; but now I'd been banned from it because of the stupid cancer.

I averted my eyes down to my chest area, the iridescent lines across my silicone blobs of flesh plopped up through my skin where my boobs used to be. They sent my head spiraling: You're deformed now. Kyle stopped wanting to fuck you and now most guys will too. You're a monster. You're not a woman anymore. It was hard enough being a non-traditionally attractive woman before this. Now you're a full freak. Good luck bitch, good luck finding anyone who will want to marry you, let alone date you, let alone fuck you, let alone find you attractive once they look under your shirt.

These feelings were internalized and nothing new. I had expressed them to myself and unfortunately, Kyle, incessantly. I'd expressed insecurities to friends, but not to the extent I had him; verbalizing it couldn't have helped. Sometimes, I hold such thoughts close to my cancer-surviving chest and keep them there, but those I fuck, I can tell them all for some reason. As long as they're someone I like.

Between drinks and tears at the Airbnb, I Google Image searched the word *Sicily*, producing pictures of turquoise tubs surrounded in green mountains, brown cliffs kissing puffy clouds, little wooden boats painted red and blue like toys. Pink and coral houses hanging off cliffs surrounded by tropical flowers. Historic ruins with volcanoes in the background. Then I dived into Sicily's darker history: images from the 1990s revealed mountains of trash about the city, piling up to make it look like the third world country some of my relatives described it as. While my grandma herself had never set foot in Sicily, or Europe for that matter, her mother fled from Prizzi, a small hillside town, whose name is derived from the Greek word Pyrizo, meaning incendiary or designed to cause fires. Many centuries ago, it was used as a point for fighting off enemy invaders and served as a hill to send smoke signals from.

Later, it's where my great grandmother was born, before she was plopped onto a boat at age 12 without a guardian, save a few other young female relatives, and told to go make it in America. The way my mom described Sicily during my great grandmother's time made it sound void of opportunities, a barren spot for any wish of succeeding in life, education, or career. Still, a part of her yearned to go back and witness its beauty.

I was raised thinking of Sicily as very poor and somewhat violent. When I was taught this in my youth, it was a fairly accurate description. In May of 1992, anti-Mafia magistrate Giovanni Falcone, his wife Francesca Morvillo, and three police escort agents were blown up by a gigantic bomb lodged under a highway not far from Palermo. A half ton of explosives, leftovers from World War II bombs, were placed between the city and its airport; a Mafia orchestrated attack. In July of the same year, another anti-mafia official named Paolo Borsellino and five members of his police escort were blown up by a bomb as he walked through the front entrance of the Palermo apartment building where his mother lived.

I had vague memories of relatives talking about all this, but mostly remember wearing a hot pink puffy jacket, riding a hot pink bike, and trying to convince my brother to ask Santa for Littlest Pet Shop toys because I thought I was too old, at nine, to admit liking them.

It was the same year my neighbor told me what sex was. She was mainly correct, though no, it's not true that one stands in the shower and bleeds afterward. At least that shouldn't be a regular occurrence. My mom asked me if I knew how sex worked as I stood in our den surrounded by a mountain of my brother's stuffed animals and my legos as Salt-N-Pepa's "Let's Talk About Sex" played on the television set. It was some sort of PSA or HIV awareness special. I told her I didn't know; I didn't want to talk about it; I wanted her to stop asking so I could ask her if I could get a pet parakeet.

"Well, I should win an award for crappiest timing ever," an email from my literary agent read, "I'm sorry to hear about you and your boyfriend. I'm truly sorry that this got piled on top of that."

Make that ex-literary agent.

I felt an explosion igniting from within. I began shaking and felt trembling in my mind. I responded by sticking stuff in me in order to diffuse the bomb. I marched to the fridge and ate half a can of leftover spam. I just wanted to feel something savory, something salty, to match my feelings.

*No. No. No. Please don't.* I wanted to beg her to take me back. *I can't lose both my marital future and my writing future.* I was feeling desperate to not be dumped by anyone of any kind. I told Kyle what happened.

"What a bitch," he said.

He talked about my agent in the same manner friends would bitch about *him* when he wouldn't fuck me. It had been about ten days since our breakup, and I'd only told one friend. I was too embarrassed to tell the rest. I'd been lying to them, lying to myself, saying it had gotten better. I even told a friend that Kyle and I had sex again, that things were looking up in the intimacy department. We hadn't. It had been months and months and months.

We had been broken up for over a week, but I was still living there, trying to figure out what to do next, hoping it would all just figure itself out.

"I'm not kicking you out," Kyle told me from his computer chair, craning his neck toward me while his eyes stayed glued to the screen, "but you do have to figure out where to go. I'm not gonna be an asshole about it but you can't stay here much longer."

Just months earlier, he told me that we'd never have to move again; just once into the house and we'd hire movers for that process.

"I'll figure it out after my camping trip," I said.

"That's fine Bucky," he said, then began complaining about having to pay full rent.

Bucky was his nickname for me. It was because we used to sing along to music with chicken noises. Now it just sounded so non-feminine and non-sexual, like a chicken getting its head cut off.

As I drove to the campsite, I thought about what to do next. Perhaps living in Italy for a bit wouldn't be a bad idea. Those photographs I'd been looking at were stunning. I'd also been teaching myself some Italian through Duolingo. Plus, I'd started the process of applying for citizenship, since the country is so lenient on that whole thing. As long as your great-grandparents weren't nationalized when they had your grandparents, you're good, in theory. Maybe I could learn about my distant past to figure out my future.

I arrived alone at the campsite with the gear Kyle bought us for this exact trip. I parked my car under a tunnel of tall trees boasting a butterfly of changing leaves. I walked upon a trail of red, orange, and yellow, an explosion of Vermont's picturesque foliage.

Being in the woods will be good, I figured. It will further prevent me from rage texting Kyle because there will be no phone reception, no way to send texts I'll later be embarrassed by, I told myself, walking toward the campsite. The sky was now fading into a warm pink. I saw familiar heads encircling a small fire.

"Hey Gina."

"Hey."

"Hi! Great to see you!"

I exchanged hugs with my old roommate and her fiancé. I hugged their friends, who are also my friends to a lesser degree, and former coworkers. Most of us had worked at the same television station in Burlington at some point. Primarily in production.

"Where's Kyle?" someone asked.

I sighed, looking into the fire, where a friend was waving a piece of meat above the flames.

Food, yes, I should have brought food.

I had brought alcohol; a six pack, a bottle of vodka, and a bottle of whiskey, but little else. If Kyle were with me, we'd be prepared and have come with food. Though he probably would have just canceled the trip. Like when my longtime friend, Chinga, came to town and Kyle canceled an hour before. It sucked. I'd spent so much time with his family. He never even met mine, mostly because my brother lived across the country in San Francisco and my parents were professional skeletons in the afterlife. He'd only met a few friends I'd made later in life. Chinga had known me since I was 10, technically.

"We broke up," I shrugged in response to the unavoidable question. "It's for the best," I added, trying to alleviate sympathy. "It wasn't working out."

"What happened?"

There were too many people around.

"A lot and also nothing, I guess," I joked, "He left me for *World of Warcraft*, aka the other woman. The other elf."

My paired-off friends shed away as the night went on, to their shared air mattresses and sleeping bags in lean-tos and tents. I began spilling it all to a single man, a friend of my friends. I don't even remember what he looks like now but he was nice to me at that moment, so it worked. Soon enough, I was on his lap, drinking moonshine or whatever out of his thermos and next thing he was going down on me on top of a blanket in a lean-to.

After getting off, I slipped off to the spot I was sharing with a couple, friends of mine, and went to sleep. Going down on people during camping isn't the cleanest sounding thing but if he was game, sure. I didn't tell him about my cancer surgery and he didn't see me with my top off. I assumed he wouldn't want to touch me.

Still, I got off knowing that from what he did know of me, he was attracted. But, I reminded myself, many guys will fuck anything. Some guys. And, nothing is as fun as fucking someone I like. I didn't know him enough to like him.

I *need* to fuck someone I like.

## David

I decided I knew who I liked and wanted to fuck.

I messaged my friend David on Facebook.

"I have just joined the singles club. Kyle and I broke up and I am a WRECK! Let's get a drink soon! I have to decide if I'm staying in Vermont and want to see as many friends as possible in case I don't."

The last line was true, with a bit of a lie attached. I didn't particularly care about seeing *all* my friends before I left. In fact, the idea scared me. I dreaded having to explain my situation over and over to people: why we broke up, what I was going to do now. It was as mundane and boring as endlessly repeating one's life story to Tinder matches. Who cares? If we fuck, or I want to fuck you, we'll end up talking about that stuff. Or if I love you enough platonically.

David sad-liked my message.

He said he'd love to meet up and we picked a day the next week in Waterbury, not far from my temporary residence. My friend Rebecca was letting me crash at her and her husband's house in a very scenic central Vermont mountainside. I brought a few suitcases over. When I arrived she said, "Honey you're home."

"Stay as long as you like," she told me. Hours after the camping trip, I texted Rebecca and told her, "We broke up. Is there any way to stay there for a week?"

"This is your home," she said.

"Thank you! I won't stay long," I promised via text. "I just need a place to come down a bit more, calm down and be away from Kyle. Plus, Amelia wants to spend time with her feathered brothers."

Amelia's full brother from another litter, a tricolor named Frankie, and her brother-in-spirit, a black and brown cavalier named Gus, lived there. Like a collection of Pokémon, I figured the furry creatures could help me through this letdown. Yes, the worst part was over, the part where I was hysterically crying for days alone in an AirBnb way too big for just me and my little dog. But I knew I was still in the bad part and that the bad part would likely be for quite a while. So, I needed to fuck someone I liked.

And I needed to figure out what to do with my newly-stitched up body. I canceled what was supposed to be my final surgery, since I was going to be a nomad and in no mental condition to undergo surgery. So I was done. The non-boob boobs would be as good as they could be for now and they were going to get some ink.

At Rebecca's, while she and her husband slept, I emailed Esme, a tattoo artist with whom I'd been discussing mastectomy coverup ideas. Then I got to looking for places in Palermo, including searches for the surrounding areas, which were cheaper and more pastoral: greens on sea greens. I settled on Bagheria. It looked rural and seaside and was just 400 a month. It was close to Palermo, just about 6 miles away. I could always take a taxi into the city if I needed to, I figured. Hmm, maybe I could do a month in Palermo and a month in Bagheria. A month exploring the city and a month in a peaceful, sleepy seascape.

A few nights in, I booked my trip, then left Rebecca's house to go meet up with David. Driving down the tree-brimmed, slopey dirt-road, I reflected on our friendship. We'd had drinks in the same manner two years earlier, just weeks before Kyle. At the time, I wondered if David and I could, or should, date. After Kyle pursued me first, David and I met up again. He too had started seeing someone. He showed me a picture. To me, she looked like a modern day Angelina Jolie in her Billy Bob Thornton era.

But, he had concerns. She was a cancer survivor, he confided in me just weeks before I was diagnosed.

"What if she gets it again and dies? It's hard for me to get attached."

With cancer comes baggage, and trust me, I knew that guys already thought I came with a lot of baggage. Now there was an extra suitcase with the word *survivor* on it.

♥

I recognized David upon entering the basement Waterbury bar, his sandy blonde hair on the back of his head a familiar image from when we worked together.

We hugged hello.

"Oh wow. Almost didn't recognize you with your dark hair."

"Oh right." I had just a few months prior dyed my blonde hair black. Most of my life I've been a blonde. Much of my life I'd been a platinum blonde. Cliché as it sounds, I went dark because I wanted a change.

"It looks good," he said with a toothy smile. Hair follicles popping through the skin around his chin, just slightly, tempted me to touch.

"Sorry I'm late," I said, wrapping my black leather purse-strap around the hook under the bar, looking down at the cocktail in his hand, which I assumed was a whiskey coke.

"You're not. I'm early. What do you want?"

"A whiskey coke?"

Soon, we were deep into a vent fest that felt deflating.

"So," I repeated my joke, "basically, my boyfriend left me for *World of Warcraft*."

"Ah, Ginaaa."

"I don't know what to fucking do with myself."

We talked about both our recent breakups as he too was recently dumped.

"I really, I am open to change," I said, wondering if I was complaining too much. "If I was doing something wrong, I know I have my flaws, I went to therapy when he told me I needed it. And I improved how I talked to him. But he wouldn't go to therapy with me. He said he was fine."

"Well, look, it sounds like you were honest with him and you tried your best to be open. Not a lot of people do that."

I thought back to another ex I was open and honest with, letting him know before an outing if I had a romantic history with someone, so that if he felt it he would know why. It was supposed to be a sign of respect. He thought it was to make him jealous. He didn't understand my logic.

David repeated, "I'm sure it's for the best."

I smiled and gave him a gentle hug.

"Thank you. I know, it just really sucks to have the idea of family right in front of your face, only to have it taken away from you."

I could sense David getting uncomfortable. *Getting too dark, Gina. Getting too fucking dark.*

"I'm gonna miss his mom more than him," I laughed. "Like, one of my other exes, I don't think about him at all, don't even remember what sex with him was like at all, but his mom's cooking, oh I remember that like it was five minutes ago."

He paid for my drink, actually drinks, which led me to think things were going the way I wanted. We hugged goodbye and he told me I could stay at his house if I ever needed a place to crash.

Jackpot. I think he does indeed like me. Well, I know he likes me as a person but this means he wants to have sex with me. This could be the rebound I need, I thought. What better way than to fuck around with someone I actually like and am attracted to? Someone I care about as a friend.

Again, I like fucking people I like.

I got home and looked at my reflection in the mirror of the guest bathroom while washing my face.

Does my skin look brighter? Is it because I got male attention? Or am I losing weight? Hmm. I definitely stopped eating as much post-breakup. I can't remember eating basically anything at all in that Airbnb. Perhaps it's because I dropped the pills. Those cursed antidepressants. I pulled up my shirt and looked at my stomach area. I did look a little lighter. I could still see a few scars from where I got lipo just months earlier, in an attempt to make the boob area look better. I'd gone from 120 to 140 without adding extra to my diet. I was becoming more than convinced it was the SSRIs. I went on them because I felt out of control of my body and my life, but they further spiraled that. Now it was time to try to get in the driver's seat on my body again.

Days later, I suggested to David over Facebook Messenger we do Halloween together. He would later tell me that this was how he knew we would hook up. I felt birds in my stomach just thinking about meeting up with him. It's only fitting that I had butterfly barrettes in my hair; I was dressed up as Jenny McCarthy from *Singled Out* with 90s multicolor pants, the palette primarily pink, and a transparent white bell sleeve top with a tie in the middle. The shirt was a souvenir from my trip to Puerto Rico, one of several vacations I took in the months leading up to the breakup, sans Kyle, where I tried to find joy in my life because my relationship was lacking so much of it. I'd find joy, and sometimes even fantasize about cheating on those trips, but never did. When I got home, Kyle would pick me up from the airport, and he'd reveal that he'd gone out on the town for the first time in months (despite my pleading for us to exist outside the home), and hung out with women. If I said anything I was classified as jealous.

My friend Krystal, a law professor, came with me on most of these trips. I always explain that when I first met her in 2010, I was shocked to learn she was a lawyer because she was just so sweet. Having grown up in a blue collar town, I always thought all lawyers were predatory and slimy. The first of these vacations we took was to Iceland. I booked that trip after Kyle confessed he wasn't planning to propose anytime soon.

David and I went to a Halloween party in the Vermont College of Fine Arts dorms, where several of my peers from grad school lived. I felt glad I had a boyfriend to live with when I attended school just months earlier, but now was wishing I'd been solo and living in the dorms with these folks. But that would have been a nightmare with cancer; who would have milked my drains? I would've been a burden, a walking symbol of pain. Now that pain was in the past, like a shadow that hung over me invisibly. David and I drank and conversed. After, we briefly went to some basement punk show, then had a few drinks in a bar where some of

Kyle's friends worked - Vermont is small. One smiled at me and we exchanged pleasantries, the kind that reeked of, "how odd of her to be here with another man at this hour but, none of my business."

"Soon you'll be in Italy doing your *Eat Pray Love* tour," David said as the warm wood of the bar kissed my pores.

I laughed and placed my arms on the bar, leaning my body toward it.

"There will be eating, but there certainly won't be any praying or loving. God, I fucking hope not on the love. I'm all set with that."

He laughed.

"Maybe more 'Eat, fuck, write about murder'" he said.

"Yes, that'll be the most likely version of things," I laughed.

He reached toward me and grabbed a strand of my black hair.

"And you'll fit in as a Sicilian with this hair. How long will you be there?"

"Two months. Last weekend I booked a month in Palermo, and then I booked a month in a tiny town called Bagheria. The second place is real cheap."

He nodded slowly and smiled.

"What about Amelia?"

"Oh, I'm bringing her too!"

"Fancy dog!"

"She will get to go to more countries than my parents in her life."

"And a lot of people." He rubbed his glass with his finger, gently. "You wanna crash at my place tonight?"

The butterflies in my hair suddenly shifted to my alcohol-soaked belly. I nodded.

He paid and we went back in his ancient car, an old 90s Honda that rode low to the ground. I told him the car was hot. When we got back to his place, I asked, "Where will I sleep?"

I damn well knew where I would *likely* end up sleeping if he didn't know I'd had cancer. But perhaps he wasn't interested. I was self-conscious.

"You can crash on the couch," he said. "Or..,"

He paused with hesitation.

"You could crash with me."

I could tell by the look in his eye that he wanted to have sex with me. All leftover doubts peeled away like an onion.

"Want some sweatpants?" he asked as we entered his room. I accepted. His bedroom had a warm glow about it. There were no curtains or blinds on the windows, so the orange-lights from the street created an almost-fireplace effect.

I kept my bra and tank on but took off the sheer top, and slipped into his baggy sweats. They were so large on me, a reminder that I'm not as big or tall as I often think. Standing next to him felt like he was at my physical level, but he, and they, never are.

We watched some episode of some show in his bed. I paid little attention to the plot. I was just staring at the screen itself, waiting for us to make out. At the episode's conclusion, he shut the laptop screen and put his arm over my shoulder and drew close. We began kissing and immediately I felt that pull, that electrical pull you feel when you're about to fuck someone you like. Finally! It felt like fleshy magnets.

He pulled his bulky sweatpants off my legs and began touching me. Then he pulled my tank top over my head. I was scared he was going to take off my bra, but he didn't. He took off everything except.  What a relief. His tongue intertwined with mine, his hands all over my body, he abruptly stopped.

"Should we fuck?"

I laughed. "Yes, I think we should!" We continued kissing.

Soon I experienced the feeling of being filled up, being close to somebody I liked. And damn, I forgot how good that could feel. We collapsed into each other's arms by the open window. The nearby house and moonlight illuminated our bodies.

Just lying there cuddling felt so warm, so comforting. It had been so long since I connected with someone in that specific way. I would always ask Kyle to lay down in bed with me, but he'd play video games instead. Sometimes he would give in to my pleading and come tuck me in, like a goddamn parent. I'd beg him to stay with me for just a few minutes. It wasn't for sex. Really, if he didn't want to fuck me again that would have sucked but it would have been fine if only we could be in bed and talk and just connect. Even watch a television show together and laugh about it.

That's really all I'd wanted. For over a year.

That's it, I decided. I'm only fucking creative people like David from now on. Artists of any kind, they know what they're doing. They get me, even if they aren't always the most stable. Fuck trying to fuck a stable person with a stable job. I like fucking people I like.

And then, the next day, it was like, BOOM. Ah, the old sex hangover, the kind that makes me think I can only date while under heavy sedation because I can't handle the feelings that come with it.

A serotonin comedown. What was first a rush of good feelings, of dopamine, of connection, now halted by the harsh reality of morning. The sun in my eyes. Smeared eye makeup. Discolored foundation over my acne patch. A hangover, a headache. The feeling of not having your sunglasses the next day. The feeling, that familiar fucking feeling of a Halloween walk of shame. Memories of walking blocks in Williamsburg, in Montreal, in Bushwick, the morning after, in stockings, in a wig, feeling slimy inside and out.

That feeling of emptiness, of shame that I don't feel naturally. It doesn't necessarily come from the inside but the outside: what people have been telling me to feel about sex my whole life, at least about casual sex, that I *should* feel shame. There were also the residual effects of forming such a bond with someone that makes you want to see them again, fuck them again. The cloudiness you feel following moments of total clarity within the pillows. After sex with someone I like, it's like bang, a bomb goes off inside my ovaries and I just want to be consumed by that person. Devoured.

I felt such an urge to contact David hours after I left his home. I texted him a screenshot of a toilet picture from Facebook, which I captioned with "Psshh it doesn't even have a bidet on it." I followed up a little later, "(and yes this is my standard post-hook up talk: toilets)."

We had bonded over bidets before we hooked up. We both had an attachment.

Soon after, I saw that he read it but didn't message back.

🎧

There were so many dry, desert days living with Kyle. I'd watch porn and think about how fun it would be to have sex again. I would do this with him in the other room, night after night, shooting people to death on his computer as I lie in bed, hoping he'd come be next to me so I could feel close to him again. Sometimes, I'd wake up and look toward the windows to the right. When I saw the only light illuminating the peach curtains was the apartment complex's parking lot streetlamp, I knew it was the middle of the night. I'd turn to the left and grab my phone off my night table. 2 or 3 or 4 am or 1 am or 3:24 am and I'd get out of bed like a child and walk into Kyle's computer room, standing shyly by the doorway.

I'd stomp, because he had his headphones on, and because if I crept up behind him and touched his shoulder he would gasp and grab his neck in terror.

He would crane his neck and lean back in his leather office chair. It would always squeak.

"I thought you said you were coming to bed tonight."

"Just a bit longer."

"Can you at least tuck me in?"

"Okay, just a minute."

Then I'd wait in our stupid queen-sized bed, on my side, the only side I ever rolled around on anymore. It was always much longer than a minute. My head back on the pillow, I'd look up at the ceiling and think about the stick-on stars in my childhood bedroom and how that felt just like this. Waiting for a parent to tuck me, being scared of the dark. Wishing they'd stay for just a few more minutes or let me leave the light on.

Then, Kyle would come in, breathless and restless.

"Please Kyle, just lay with me for a few more minutes, until I fall asleep."

"I can't, my Bucky" he said, kissing my forehead and patting my side. "Goodnight, I love you."

"I love you," I'd say, but it felt forced.

It *was* forced. On both sides. I knew he didn't love me anymore. I could *feel* it. Like a visceral punch to the gut.

I stewed in anger recalling all this in Rebecca's guest room. The bed was warm and inviting like in a grandmother's bedroom. I faced a desk stacked with awards. The room was chilly, so I got out of bed and put a sweatshirt on from the floor, one I'd thrown off that morning without the will to fold up or place anywhere neat. I put it on and slid back under the covers and tried to breathe slowly. Stop thinking about *him*. No more Kyle. Think about David. What good sex, I remembered. Yes, remember the fucking, please. What an awesome memory of a man clearly being attracted to me despite my new deformity. Yes, I left my shirt on during sex but he knew, to some degree, what was underneath. Think of this *please*. Why couldn't I savor that memory? Why couldn't I stew in it and all its glory? If I were a dude, having sex with David would have been a conquest, I think. But instead, here I was just simmering in anxiety about it all.

Does David like me? Of course he does, what I am fucking 12? He was just fucking me. But did he think the sex was okay? Was he weirded out about the cancer? Did I do *that* right or that right? I didn't have these thoughts during sex or in the immediate aftermath because my intuition hugged me so tightly, telling me, *he wants me, he likes me, there is a connection*. But there *was*, there was a connection, right? I knew in my intuitive heart that there was.

Still, he hadn't responded to my toilet joke. I didn't like that. I set my phone on "do not disturb" and tried to rest. An hour later, I got up and checked, still no text. Must be a mistake. I restarted my phone. I texted one of my friends who cares more about which dicks I'm touching than art, "just had the best rebound with a friend."

They were so excited for me.

"Maybe more than a friend now!" they wrote, along with a smiley face. I got it, they thought it would blossom into a relationship. How wrong they were, how wrong they almost always were. What's a friend anyway? The word is so vague. Could be someone whose last name you don't really know or someone who licks your privates from time to time.

    I suddenly felt silly for bragging about fucking someone who couldn't even find the time to text me back. No Gina. Don't be crazy. He's probably busy. Probably not ignoring you. But it wasn't a text. It was a Facebook message and he could see that you sent it. It said *read*. I must not mean as much to him as he does to me. Does he mean much to me, or did he just fuck me good and now I'm needy. He did indeed fuck me good, and I was craving more affection, even if it was through text. A text back would be an extension of the pleasure I got from the sex, the validation, the everything.

✦

You would think that after surviving cancer, the cancer itself would be the focus of my cover up tattoo session. And not boys. Not fucking. But even at the most serious times, sex and hopes of love have found a way to take priority.

I went to see Esme, whose shop was located above a t-shirt store in Montpelier, a day after the toilet text. Two days after sex with David. The parlor was comfy and warm, as was her presence.

"How's Kyle?" she asked.

Vermont is small and her ex-husband worked with Kyle. She was just making small talk.

I smiled and shrugged. "He's okay."

She looked up at me with knowing eyes.

"We broke up," I blurted out. "But it's okay. It's for the best."

I added a lie: "It's amicable."

I mean was it a lie, though? We weren't yelling at each other. I wasn't even expressing to him how the breakup made me feel. If I did, he would just tell me I was acting abusive.

My brain didn't want to go there, so it obsessed over David instead: why hasn't he texted me back? Is he freaked out? Is he grossed out by my body, scared of me being a cancer survivor? My hurricane mind continued to swirl.

These thoughts enveloped me while Esme drew an outline of flowers over where my nipples once were. Watching the transformation of my scar into something ornamental was invigorating. I looked more human. And, better yet, the inking didn't hurt at all. I guess losing nerve endings in that area paid off in that department. I did feel something, a tingling, numb sensation, like using a vibrator for too long, pulsing though random areas of my body.

As I listened to the buzzing, feeling the strange sensations, I got almost angry at David, feeling a tinge of betrayal.

I did not want to be treated like this. My past insistence for respect had led to Kyle calling me abusive, because I didn't want to be the victim of abuse and was pre-emptive about it, perhaps to the point of becoming abusive myself. For years of my life, I was a pushover. I let guys cheat, lie, invade my privacy, and beat me. I never even insulted them. The ones who didn't mistreat me, I'd travel so far for. I would take a metro ride and two buses. I'd always travel so far for affection and they never came out to see me. I never questioned the fairness of it. After a time, it hurt too much. Then I traveled as far as I could to avoid it. More than a few buses. It was hard to turn back.

I would not be mean to David, I vowed. But it had been 24 hours. I had to know that he wasn't just using me for sex, and that he wasn't repulsed by the sex. I needed this affirmation. I must tell him this with caution and rationality. I would be calm and mature and compose myself like the talented, successful, desirable adult that I clearly am.

That all went to the wind within seconds. I wrote back "RUDE" as soon as Esme took a break to use the bathroom. It's just that suddenly there were these storm clouds in my brain, just fogging up the place. I saw text bubbles brewing in our chat almost immediately. Was he annoyed with me? Would he tell me to fuck off? Would he think I'm being crazy? I felt tingling in my chest, butterfly barrettes breaking.

"Yeah, very rude to his guests indeed," he wrote.

Oh, he thought I was talking about the toilet. Oh good. And yeah, he probably just forgot to text back.

Still the message was vague. I scrolled back at all our texts. This was just the way we talked over social media. I'd just have to see him again. And see in person if he enjoyed fucking me or if he was so put off by me, by my surgeries, by cancer, that he wouldn't ever want to again.

I wrote back another joke about the toilet. All was fine, but was it just because I made it *seem* fine? Great, I was obsessing.

Why am I like this? And will I ever feel stable enough to date again?

◻

    Once those feelings of intensity over David finally subsided, a bit anyway, I felt flatline, watching intense people arguing on reality shows with Rebecca and her husband. In the course of one evening, we flipped through clips of *Vanderpump Rules, Jersey Shore, Real Housewives. The Real Housewives of New York* was the best because by this point none of them were married anymore and they were all going through real life shit. Each and every episode was jam packed with drama and they didn't need to stretch it out.

    For a while, in a very pretentious manner, I admit, I decided I would have no internet or television in my house. This decision was as much based on poverty as snobbery. I was a reporter at the local paper, making a meager wage and also wanted to focus my time at home writing, or reading, which was just research for more writing. But that fucking sucked, so I spent as much of my free time when I would be doing that studious stuff at their house watching TV. The reality shows were more inspiring than a dry book. That's when I became a big-time fan of reality shows again. This time it stuck and I no longer hate on people for things that bring them joy.

    We'd drink wine from her decanter and sit on the house's bottom floor and watch Ronnie and Sammi Sweetheart fight. All that couple did was either fuck in bed or fight in bed and go to clubs only to fight and go back to the crusty reality show home and fight and cry in bed again. Sometimes Ronnie would tear the bed apart and throw her clothes off the balcony.

    It made me feel good about my own failed relationship. Yeah, it was a mess, but it wasn't a mess *like that.* As Sammi yelled at Ronnie for pushing her in the street, telling him, "You traumatized me, Ronnie!!" I saw Rebecca's eyes start to flutter. By the end of that scene, her lids were shut.

    Rebecca would often fall asleep early, then her husband would carry her up to bed.

I could hear him shoveling the driveway in the morning. He'd cook with her and do all the dishes. If she was grouchy, he'd tiptoe around her and try to cheer her up. I couldn't even get Kyle to wash the dishes while I was working full time and in school full time. I'd come home to him playing video games and a sink filled with dishes. After a 12-hour day I'd usually wash them all. When I asked him to help out more, to share the work, he'd essentially blame me for being a workaholic, which I was and probably still am.

"If you want to blame anything for the breakup, blame your cancer." His words still burned. My phone dinged. It was Gmail, alerting me Kyle had deleted our streaming account memberships. My reality show access, gone. If it were just the cancer, would he be so adamant about removing *me* like a tumor? Did he resent me?

I remembered how I resented my mom when she had cancer, for changing, for being different, for being even less warm to me than before. Was this similar? God Damnit, this was the very thing I was trying to avoid. If only I'd stuck to my guns and just dumped him and didn't let him sweet talk me into staying together during the onset. But then I wouldn't have had someone to take care of me. That was nice. He was good to me for some time. Maybe it was just too much for him. Maybe I'm too much for anyone.

Tipsy and feeling warm and tingly in my extremities I slipped under the blanket that cool November night and tipsy-texted my old friend Jon, my longtime lover who I'd been fucking on and off since 2002.

The last time Jon and I talked was about nine months prior, when I was still with Kyle. Kyle was in the computer room playing *World of Warcraft* and I was wrapped in an afghan in the lonely living room watching chunks of white snow fall from the black sky to the ground, illuminated by parking lot light. I reached out to Jon to apologize for freaking out on him for ignoring my texts in the recent past.

"I just wanted to apologize for being such a jerk the other year," I wrote. "Every now and then I think about my behavior and feel ashamed. You did not deserve that."

I got a message back nearly immediately and squinted my eyes as I gulped down a decent-sized sip of red wine from the glass in front of me before looking. Would it be rage? If so, that would have been acceptable.

"My behavior was not so great as well and I owe you an apology."

"Maybe so, but I didn't have to lash out at you the way I did."

During a two-minute rage-filled texting session, I'd completely attacked his character, even ripped on him for smoking cigarettes, something he beat himself up about. He has never, not even once, said anything unkind to me and there were a lot of opportunities for him to do so, ever since 2002 when we first locked lips as teenagers-in-heat in the back of a Toyota. I cut him out of my life when he wasn't giving me the kind of attention I arrogantly assumed I deserved. In this case, I was indeed being shitty. No doubt about it.

My rage-text session to Jon occurred just a few months before I began dating Kyle, while I was still in vicious mode.

Perhaps I felt he wasn't texting me back enough after our most recent hookup. I didn't want a relationship; Like with David, I just didn't want to feel disposable. But I felt that way in the sexual aftermath, so I thought it would be easier for me to remove *him* from *my* life like a tumor. Cruelly, as if with a knife. It didn't make things easier. It chipped away at my conscience, like carrying around an even heavier tumor. When he received my apology well, and reliably gave me one of his own, this rock of excess tissue was excavated.

But there were others still wedged inside me from my rage era. I planned to apologize to a recent ex the next day. Someone I told was dead to me. He wasn't treating me right, but he didn't deserve that. He had informed me he was bipolar and I should have been sympathetic. But it was hard at the moment. Literally one day after apologizing to Jon in 2017, I woke up to a phone call from Rebecca. She told me the person I was planning to apologize to just died of an opiate overdose. It was the only moment minus Kyle crying in the shower in 2016, that made me realize I could never be vicious again. I could be honest, and must always be honest and assertive and not put up with shit, but that does not mean I need to overreact or be unkind.

Jon lived in Northern Vermont in a home so far north it was basically on the Canadian border. He spent his nights in the upstairs bedroom of a little farmhouse on a dirt road in a picturesque and windy hill. The house itself was so close to the road it was nearly kissing it, no, licking it. And it was on a bend, practically begging for a drunk driver to smash into a bedroom. I pulled up to his place, greeted by snow in the grooves of the driveway between the mud and grass.

Of course there's snow, Gina. It's Vermont. Never be surprised by the snow. I grew up in this world. Why am I ever surprised by the coldness of it?

Cut scene to the interior of Jon's house: us getting drunk, shots of Fireball like kids. Shots of Jack Daniels. Then we ordered pizza. Then we messed around in his room. I left my bra on.

"Hey, I'm sorry again for what came between us before," he said with his head resting on my covered chest. I looked down at him, immediately conscious of my deformity, thinly veiled by black cotton.

"It's okay." I stroked his hair.

I took a breath so big I could feel it move his head.

"Why did you get freaked out and like, ignore my texts? Were you worried I wanted a relationship?"

"Yeah," he said. "And I felt like I had nothing to offer you. I mean look at my life. I still haven't gotten my license back. I don't have my shit together."

"But, what on earth did I text you which indicated to you that I wanted a relationship?"

"I'm not sure." He giggled. It was funny to him. Perhaps he realized the absurdity of assuming himself a prize.

"I don't think I texted you anything that would lead to that, in my opinion."

"Yeah," he said.

"All I did was like, text a joke or two within a day or two of us having sex. I didn't want a relationship with you."

"Oh."

"I just like to treat the people that I have sex with like people, with respect."

"Yeah that's fair."

I rolled my eyes.

"Why do guys assume that women always want a relationship?"

He responded by going down on me.

♣

I just had to fuck David again before leaving the country.

We were up in his bedroom within minutes my arrival. I was wearing high waisted pants with a belt built into them and a shirt with an ungodly amount of ties. He looked confused by the outfit, so I burst out, "I love wearing clothing like this when I know I'm going to hook up with a dude. Because they aren't sure if they are supposed to compliment it as they struggle to take it off."

David laughed, "I'll take the struggle."

He managed to remove my shirt, then politely pushed me to take off my bra.

"Are you sure?"

"Oh come on Gina, of course."

As soon as he pulled it away, revealing my newly tattooed flower nipples, I held my hands across my chest. He put a finger in between them, prodding me to let go.

"Come on, it's hot," he said. "You look good."

Still, I was glad the lighting in the room was dim. The scars were less obvious. I steered him away from my chest.

Soon enough, he was fucking me against the wall on his bed. I couldn't help but be loud with him. He fucked me just long enough that he left me wanting more, the perfect amount of time. Not too long, but definitely long enough! Any more might start to hurt, and leave me craving more and more of him filling me up.

"I felt like I was fucking Princess from the Mario Brothers," he said. "You're a cartoon now. Seriously, you look good. You don't need to be self-conscious about that stuff."

I smiled but my face was turned toward the wall, his words dying in the back of my neck. Then he asked, "Wanna go for a food run?"

We rode together to the grocery store in his car, like a couple of yesteryear. *My* yesteryear of me and Kyle, only more connected. Getting snacks. Or like me and male roommates of mine. Getting baked and going to the store to joke around. It's the kind of innocent fun I love most about being alive. I used to get high with Chinga when we lived in Denver together. We'd walk across the way to Walmart. We'd chuckle at a grocery store display, "Look how weird this Teddy Bear icon looks.. Look how much of a pedophile Count Chocula looks like.. Look at that man in aisle eight getting berated by his wife.." What a world. What a life! This is what being alive is all about: trolling and observing and being silly and having someone along with a sense of humor whose mirrors yours. Oh god, If I could just do that all day. I like being silly with people I like.

We decided on both pizza bagels and pizza bites for our lil' sex session. When we got back to David's, he put some of each in the oven and we sat at his kitchen table. He handed me a seltzer.

"How's the planning for Sicily coming along?"

"Oh, not bad, but it's hard to find information about the area. Like, I've been doing a lot of searching and can't really gauge how safe or dangerous it is. I mean the crime rate doesn't seem bad at all, but I found some bloggers complaining about the poverty. I wonder if there'll be a lot of beggars or whatever and how aggressive the dudes are."

"Yeah, Italians do have that rep."

"Yeah, I just wonder what that means, exactly. Like, cat calling or pushy? Dangerous?"

"Have you joined any expats groups?"

"A what now?" I asked in a jokey nasal voice. He might have missed the humor, as he was precision-lock focused on the important task at hand. If there's one thing I've learned having sex as a straight female, it's that dudes love food before and after sex. It's very important to many of them. Sorry to generalize. He peeked in the oven to check on the bagels and bites. I smelled the melting cheese. That familiar smell of slumber parties and horror films, lying on the floor in sleeping bags and hoping to somehow date a boy.

"Ex-patriots group." He sat in the chair beside me, leg wrapped in sweats touching mine wrapped in spandex.

"Ah. No I haven't." I laughed, "I don't know what an expat technically even is to be honest."

"We can look for some after we eat. I joined one when I was out in Europe and it was super helpful for making friends, for me."

"Oh cool, thanks! Yeah, I'd love that!"

"And it just means someone who left their country to live somewhere else. Like you"

The pizza bagels and bites were ready. We pulled them out and picked at guilty pleasure until it ceased to exist.

His bedroom was beginning to feel like a warm nest to me, filled with pheromones, hot breath, and blankets. Some of my butterfly barrettes from Halloween were still scattered about his desk. I saw a hot pink one on the floor by the foot of his computer chair. I pretended not to notice; I enjoyed the idea of leaving my mark behind with a bright little butterfly.

"Let's take a look." He opened up his computer.

"Travel blogs to Sicily," he said aloud, typing into Google. "Hmm, here's A British Travel Gal's Guide to the World: Sicily Edition."

"Sounds cheesy," I mumbled.

"Now, Gina, let's not be too judgemental yet." He grabbed my hip and placed me on his lap, "Okay..'The streets were dirty, there was too much poverty, the neighbors were rude and they got arrested for some kind of Mafia reason,'"

"Wow, *she* needs to be told not to be judgemental."

David laughed and continued reading, but silently.

"Wow, this woman sucks."

Next, we came across a message board for expats, also featuring a British woman complaining about the "poverty" there.

"God, how bad can it be?"

"The British are more classist than us," he said. "I'm going to search to see if we can find some poverty stats. How bad is poverty in.. where are you going again?"

"Palermo."

"Palermo," he said, typing it in. "..Poverty in Palermo. Poverty is on the rise in Italy. It's been fueled by the economic crisis, especially in the south of the country," he read aloud. "Looks like crime is down overall in Palermo. By a lot."

Then he pulled up a 2017 article from The Independent entitled "Sicily's economy is so depressed even the Mafia is moving to Germany to find jobs."

I laughed nervously.

"Look, I'm sure it's not that bad. I bet it's going to be beautiful. These British people just suck."

"Yeah imagine going to Italy and having nothing to say about the food, just complaining about 'poor people.' I hope Amelia isn't snobby like that, she is of British blood.'"

"Just try not to date any Mafia dudes," he laughed as he slid his hand up my side and over the back of my neck, gently massaging the area where my neck and shoulder connect on my right side. He began rubbing in circles, almost instinctively where my tension typically settles. It was like he was waving sage all over my broken chakra or aura or whatever you believe.

We had sex again. I woke up to snow falling as I slipped out of his bed to pick up all my items of clothing: socks here, undies there, and my jeans all in a pile there. Snow. It was time to leave this cold place and try to become warmer.

## Palermo

Days before flying to Sicily, I saw a friend in New York City. We got a table in a candlelit restaurant in Brooklyn with brick walls and Victorian paintings and overpriced cocktails.

After a few drinks, she grabbed for my hands over the table with tears in her eyes. "I know you're resilient, but I just, it's just about time you had something good happen in your life."

It was so sweet that it made me very, very uncomfortable.

"It's fine," I said robotically as she cried. "I'm sure, you know, I mean I'm the common denominator, right? Like, clearly I am doing something wrong. Or putting off bad energy or whatever." I was already pretty toasty by this point, the warmth of the wine swimming around my body like goldfish.

"No," she exclaimed. "You're one of the most thoughtful people I know. You're a good person, and you deserve love."

I thought of all the not-so-thoughtful people I knew who had boyfriends and husbands whom I'd personally seen act more distant than I or dramatic or mean or shitty to their dudes than I ever had in private to my exes.

"Maybe it's not about being a good person," I said. "I mean, it's not. Life doesn't owe anyone anything. Just because I've had things bad, doesn't mean that I'm *due* for good. Quite the opposite. If anything, it just means I'm due for more crap, *because* I'm traumatized I won't be able to receive good things in the same way as people who haven't gone through the same things. I'm too scared. It's too high stakes. A boyfriend symbolizes possibly a replacement of family, and I, that's just too much for me to deal with. The risk is too high for me. The fall from the breakup tree is going to break my whole body when I fall, not just the heart. It could be a fall from a low hanging branch. It was before. Now it feels like I'm almost all the way up the tree. I just can't fucking do it."

My drunken, mumbling monologue made my friend, my beloved yet sheltered friend, cry even more.

A drink later though, the mood was much more jovial.

"Maybe you can write about it," she said. "Traveling to Italy. So cool."

I shrugged and laughed. I didn't see why I would. Everything seemed so flatline. I felt so flatline. There didn't seem to be much weight to the trip, nothing sticky. I had spent so much time trying to touch the ground by being with Kyle, trying to fasten myself to something, but ended up floating around aimlessly in space instead. It felt like I was still hovering there. Everything I did appeared meaningless, with little footing in my actual desires and needs.

I told her all my stuff was now in a storage unit up in Vermont, how snow was surrounding the cube.

"One of the best things that ever happened to me was getting a storage unit," she said. "I met my now-husband just months later. You should get a tattoo of a storage unit, because trust me, it's the best thing for your life. Soon you will find your soulmate too, like I did."

She was a true Gilbert-like character, and I knew in my heart, always has been. She enjoys rom-coms and hates horror. She's a real woman, the kind who stars in Hallmark movies, who people care about when they go missing. I'm not destined for such things. Always knew it; always will.

In order to bring Amelia, I had to make her fit in a 11W x 16L x 8H little bag. When I picked it up at Petsmart, I got the roomiest one available, but when I brought it home it apparently was not roomy enough. Amelia looked at it with sad, almost knowing eyes. Perhaps she was also bewildered by how she would fit. At least it was soft. The top only came about to Amelia's shoulders. She may be just a petite 15 pounds, but is lanky and long legged. I unzipped the top of the bag and stuck her in. She instinctively stuck one of her paws back out. I placed it back in. She stood there and sulked. I unzipped her right side of it to unveil breathing holes and tried to gently push her hand down so I could zip the top. She looked like an uncomfortable giraffe crammed into a box. By the time I coaxed her head lower and zipped the top, she looked miserable. I picked her up.

Oh boy, I thought.

"At least you have a sedative for her," my stepmom, Ann, told me. She was kind enough to let me stay with her for a few weeks before flying off.

Yes. She may need that.

I unzipped the top and freed Amelia from the meshy contraption.

"Sorry baby dog," I said. She immediately went from a sulking baby to frolicking around the living room.

I could already tell this was going to be a problem. If I had someone with me, it would be funny and cute. But alone, I'd be struggling. I toyed with the idea of dragging my stepmom along to Italy. God knows I needed the support.

"I just realized," Ann told me, sipping a glass of white wine. "You're gonna be over there for the holidays. Won't you be lonely?"

I hadn't even factored the holidays into the equation.

I shrugged.

"That's fine. I've had worse holidays, for sure."

Ann laughed. She knew very well of the time I spent Christmas in a psychiatric ward in 2010, just a couple months after being sexually assaulted by a serial rapist. I was already self-medicating my pain with cocaine, numbing my senses, but the rape was the catalyst that kicked me into a full-blown mental health crisis. Soon enough, I was smuggling drugs on a plane to withstand the trip to my high school reunion, to which I wore a fucking wedding dress to add some more sprinkles of cliche, before checking into a detox center, only to be encouraged by family to get out and get back to work. Work. Work. Work. I worked myself back into crisis and checked into the psychiatric ward on Christmas Eve.

It was all a joke now, being in the psych ward on Christmas, because *I* made it a joke. And I wrote a book about it, therefore I overcame it, as they say. I had grown accustomed to "overcoming things" through work, through my writing, so much that it became a crutch. I wasn't sure I could handle walking through the world without it.

I worked the day I flew to Italy because my flight was at 5 p.m. I figured I could handle it. But it just happened to be the day the area district attorney's office released hours worth of material in a family annihilation case. The Chris Watts case. So, en route to the airport, with Amelia in the bag on the floor of an Uber next to me, I turned my hotspot on and pulled my laptop out onto my lap like a douche, and reviewed the materials and worked late. It was important! Right?

I wrote line after line about a dead woman, who like me, should be in the midst of a breakup. But she didn't have the opportunity to ruminate and eventually move forward. Instead, her selfish husband killed her and took their kids down too. I remembered talking with an expert on the phenomenon of family annihilators for a story once. She told me that often, killers don't view their partner or even their kids as separate from them, but as an extension of themselves. So despite the undeniable fact of murder, it's a weird and warped form of suicide too. Typically, it's men who commit this crime.

When we got to the terminal, I carried Amelia in her cramped bag along with my purse crammed with my laptop and makeup. I lugged around my 27" x 21" x 14" suitcase, which I would be checking. It proved difficult to hold both my dog and bag while dragging the suitcase. Damn it, this is why I need to be in a relationship! These kinds of reasons and these reasons only. I sat in the airport, continuing to work until boarding began. Even then, I let others in before me. I wanted to finish up as much as possible before shutting down for a while.

On the first plane, which was the longest ride, from New York to Milan, I got on and all these people with accents smiled at Amelia.

"There's an extra seat for her. She can sit up here when we inna the air," a woman said.

Damn, Italians really do love their dogs.

With my legs pinned up against the plastic seat in front of me, I started watching *The Notebook*, a film I'd never seen. I like watching romantic comedies on planes. The rage they ignite inside me provides enough entertainment to survive the boring flight. I get so jittery, restless, in the air that I need something soft and light to hold my attention. Sometimes I fall for the stories too. I can be sappy on occasion, particularly on airplanes.

As the movie started, the main stud Noah falls so hard for Allie when he first sees her that he just *has* to possess her. Then he threatens suicide as he dangles from a ferris wheel until Allie agrees to go on a date with him. Threats of suicide upon first glance in one of the most romantic films of my generation, huh? In reality, someone who acts that way ends up beating you or trying to control you, *not* being a sweetheart. It made me think of family annihilators.

I didn't finish the movie. Instead, I turned to the music on the screen in front of me and listened to "7 Rooms of Gloom" by The Four Tops. I listened to it for about an hour and half, dissociating, petting Amelia through her soft crate as she repeatedly attempted to break out.

*"I see a house, a house of stone*
*A lonely house, 'cos now you're gone*
*Seven rooms, that's all it is, seven rooms of gloom*

*I live with emptiness, without your tenderness*
*You took the dream I had for us, and turned that dream into dust*

*I watch a phone that never rings, I watch a door that never rings*
*I need you back into my life and turn this darkness into light*

*I'm all alone in this house, turn this house into a home"*

Listening to music while moving through the air helped me think, like showering or driving. I felt comfortable at this point, but dreaded being alone in Milan for seven hours with Amelia. What if there was nowhere for her to use the bathroom?

Cut scene to Milan. There was not.

I brought her into a bathroom stall and took her out.

"Go pee," I said. Usually, she listens to this, but we're on grass or sidewalk, not inside. She knows she's not supposed to pee on the inside. Yeah, it was shitty to try to get her to pee on the floor, but what other choice did I have? Have her stomach or bladder or whatever explode?

She just looked at me with wide eyes, confused.

✈

When I arrived in Palermo, I waited for my checked luggage to show up on the carriage. A black suitcase with a red ribbon. I saw a lot of black suitcases come out and trolley around me. Eventually they all got scooped up. Not mine. Soon the crowd dissipated, until it was just me and two men standing feet apart. I was clutching Amelia's crate as she wriggled within. My purse was heavy and kept sliding off my shoulder.

As I heard one of the men let out a sigh of relief, I saw three lone suitcases dancing forward on the revolving metallic floor. I picked up my suitcase and wobbled it and Amelia toward security. A man who looked both like Al Pacino and a young version of my grandfather cleared me. I had read that the best way to get to the city from the airport was to take a sort of taxi caravan, which would be shared with others. No Lyft or Uber. I got into a van with several others, who all spoke Italian. We drove through unknown darkness, stopping for various people while the rest chatted in Italian to one another, for about an hour until my cross street was reached.

My apartment host informed me her housekeeper, a neighbor, would let me into the place. I just had to walk down after getting to the cross street. After getting out of the taxi van and paying the driver, I released Amelia from her crate and leashed her, trying to balance walking her with rolling my heavy suitcase down the cobbled streets of this foreign new land. I knew I looked like a tourist and hated that.

"Where is via Vittorio Emanuel?" I asked myself aloud, surveying the buildings. Everything had a sort of monotone feel to it, like walking into a movie. Also it was very dark.

I couldn't figure out which way to go. I opened Google maps and entered the street. It said, "error." Where was the street? I was at the cross-road right? Did I type the name wrong? I didn't see the sign on the street, or any sign. I turned on my phone's international plan. Sure, it would cost 10 bucks, but worth it. It was dark and I sensed people hovered around like birds. Hmm, maybe this pedestrian street is the way. I went down a cobblestone lane, passing alleyways draped with white fabrics and white Christmas lights. One was an 8-pointed star, all white with a trail behind it. It resembled the shooting star I saw when I went camping just days after the breakup.

I walked past food carts fuming with smoke and couples eating gelato and drinking wine on the street out of cups until I heard a woman ask, "Gina?"

She had strong eyelines and hair up in a bun, gray strands dangling down. She stood by an alley with the sign, "Vicolo dei Calzonai" plastered to the cement next to it. Made me think of a calzone who had a baby with a cannolo. Yum. Next to her was a young girl with dark hair and piercing green eyes. She couldn't have been any older than 11.

"Bonsoir," I said, instantly realizing I'd mistakenly spoken French.. "Um..Piacere!"

They led me through the alley. Shirts draped over lines. Boys yelled something from a top balcony and the girl went from smiling at me softly to screaming harshly in Italian, gesturing her hand at the sky, then switching back to soft.

"Do you need help?" she asked, taking my giant suitcase. She spoke English well, certainly better than I spoke Italian; my "Italian" was embarrassing, basically equivalent to a four-year-old or parrot.

"No it's okay," I said.

"Let a me help."

I handed her Amelia's leash instead.

"Grazie, millie," I said, echoing one of the few phrases I'd memorized.

I then proceeded to drag the suitcase up all four gray and ancient floors to the unit.

The woman opened the door to my place, revealing a tiny yet adorable kitchen, with a pea green fridge and fawn-colored tiles that spread beyond the kitchen and to the bedroom. I let go of the suitcase.

"Venire," the woman said as she pointed at the stove. The wall behind the stove was full of tiles itself, blue and white Mediterranean style with patterns that married geometry with flowers.

"Gas. Careful."

I nodded as my eyes locked in on the chalkboard by the fridge. It had the wifi password on it.

Then she led me to the bathroom. The shower was a stand up one, tiny, with only a petite circular curtain outlining it. I smirked at the bidet, sitting right by the toilet. She explained something about the shower I couldn't understand. I said thank you after asking three times and not getting it. I was sure I could figure it out.

I followed the woman and the girl to the bedroom: a bed with an orange bedspread and pillows. A pole above the bed held up two red pillows which leaned against the wall. I've never seen such a thing before; I presumed it was to lean against.

The girl pointed at a white air conditioner looking thing on the wall.

"Air," she said.

Then she pointed to what looked like a space heater.

"Propane." She flipped a switch and a flame ignited. She turned it off. Then she pointed to a little heater fan.

She led me out to the balcony.

"Terrazino."

It was full of succulent plants, cacti, and hanging plump greens.

"When it's a rain, you push," she said, pointing to a squee-gee broom on the balcony, gesturing pushing water off the roof. It looked like a task one of my relatives would have done in 1902 and I was amused by this.

"Okay, grazie."

"Piacere. Nice to meet you."

"Buona notte."

I parrotted them, patting myself on the back for not accidentally saying "bonsoir" again.

After they left, I sat out on the balcony, dazed.

Why am I here? Oh yeah, to get away. To eat good food, to fuck some foreign guys, and to write about murder so I can afford to do it. I guess.

I went to pee and looked up at the window while doing so; it was where the toilet paper rested. The bathroom window was literally a hole in the wall with some gate. Perhaps this would be considered archaic to that snobbish British blogger, but the bathroom was way more high-tech than basically any bathroom in the states. I couldn't wait to mention the bidet to David, who I was still thinking about.

I turned on the shower. I needed to get the airplane grime off me. Plus, I was that kind of exhausted in which I felt drunk. I climbed inside a half foot by half foot cell, tinier than any shower I'd ever been in. I surrounded myself with the curtain. It touched both my leg and my head it was so close to me. I felt like a giant. I let the hot water drip down my back as the water pressure massaged the back of my head. I let out a deep sigh. When I was almost finished, it suddenly felt like I was being stabbed in the head with icicles.

"AHH!!" I nearly slipped. The water, with no warning, switched to ice cold. I turned the knob. So this is what that kid was talking about. I reached for a towel, shivering, and wrapped it around my body. I got out shaking and searched the place for something to cover my head. I wasn't clean, but I was definitely alert. So the shower's hot water is brisk. Who cares? At least there's a bidet!

Later that night, in the orange bed, I messaged David about the bidet: "I have a bidet, what peasants the people are here to have something more advanced than rich people in our country!" I sent the joke then kept refreshing my browser until I slammed my laptop shut and put it and my phone under the bed so I'd stop being like this.

Was I trying to be too cool for him or was I being too clingy? Oh, the age old question. Was he like Jon and thought that I wanted a relationship because I was messaging him, even though I was an ocean and a sea away? I didn't want him to go away. If I kept it casual and fun, he would never go away, I told myself. Even if I was physically away, I didn't want to be abandoned again.

I got up from bed. A few minutes chilling out had helped alleviate the flight fatigue. Now it was time to unpack. I folded my clothes and hung up the others. I found a safe place to store my passport in one of the kitchen drawers, just in case. I put my driver's license in the drawer of the desk.

After I felt a bit more settled, I opened my Kindle. Ahh the Kindle. A gift for my 34th birthday from Kyle. I thought he was going to get me a ring but he gave me this instead: a Kindle with a faded brown leather protector. The protector had a nice, comforting, nostalgic feeling. I was disappointed at the time but now I thought of it as one of the best things I got out of the relationship. Oh yes, and having someone to take care of me when I had cancer. That was something I was still grateful to him for. Can't ignore that, even if I'm mad at him, I thought.

Before getting on the plane, I purchased *Brutally Honest* by Mel B, aka Scary Spice, and uploaded it into the digital, leather-bound book. A friend said it was "juicy" on my Facebook timeline and while I don't normally trust their judgment, I needed a book equivalent to Jersey Shore. Sports for women. I needed something light but not chick lit like *Eat Pray Love*. I knew from the book synopsis that Mel B. wrote about suicide attempts and fucking Eddie Murphy and drugs and abusive relationship chaos and I wanted to read all that. In a light format too? Yes please. It would be like eating an ice cream sundae full of poison.

I began looking at it and for once, for the first time in a while, I could read words like candy. Easy and obvious, not like some of the books I had to read during grad school. Or otherwise. For years now, as soon as I started trying to read it would become so difficult. I'd look at the words and not absorb them. Like I'd be so high up in the clouds in my head, despite not being high, I couldn't feel the reality of the words in front of me.

"My life was a sham," Mel B wrote. "Behind the glitter of fame, I felt emotionally battered, estranged from my family. I felt ugly and detested by the very man who once promised to love and protect me, my husband and manager, Stephen."

Okay, a very different story than my current life, I thought. But it made me feel better. Look, if Scary Spice had major boy problems and felt ugly, maybe we're all doomed, amiright?

My reading was soon interrupted by a sound from above. It sounded like scattering or, no, it was a bed squeaking. People fucking above me.

At the same time, I heard some yelling from outside. A man and a woman. It sounded like a domestic argument, like a woman from a 1950s movie about Italian Americans or something. I imagined her wearing a fucking apron and holding a rolling pin above her husband's head as she yelled things in Italian so loudly I could nearly feel it in my bones.

I read a bit more.

"He made me feel ugly."

K, relatable.

"Like a waste of space. Like I was a terrible mother, a whore. Like I was lucky to be married to him because no one else would put up with trash like me."

I remembered back in the day, way back, my ex-boyfriend calling me a whore and a bitch when he broke up with me. Then he ripped the necklace he'd given me off my neck and broke it, as well as my disposable camera. It was my first time in Europe. I was visiting him during his stint there and he told me he wasn't going to give me the satisfaction of having things picture perfect. I hadn't exactly behaved perfectly before his outburst; I admitted that I had slept with his friend. But the whole relationship had been corrupt. We were in an open relationship. He had another girlfriend and lied to both of us about the other until she reached out to me to clarify what was really going on. He'd flirt with my friends in front of me with no remorse. All the rules in the relationship basically only applied to me. Still, I did something inexcusable.

I had never verbally lashed out at a man until years after this incident. In my longest relationship ever, the man I was with didn't explicitly *say* I was ugly, he'd instead not so subtly hint at ways to improve my looks: telling me to tan, telling me to get a stylish haircut, telling me to dress nicer. There was another ex who made sure to tell me that he found me attractive despite my prominent nose, following a post-breakup drinking session with his buddies. Shortly after, as I continued to pack up my stuff from our cohabitated home, he complained that we broke up as I was getting "hotter." I always assumed it was because that bout of acne was clearing up as I got on hormonal birth control.

The bed above was still squeaking, but another kind of noise was starting to overshadow it. In the distance I heard what sounded like some sort of street party. The music, was it Spanish? Or was it Italian?

I wanted to go outside and check it out, and maybe would have if the alley didn't spook me so much and my legs weren't so tired.

But I craved the excitement of whatever was going on out there so much.

When "Despacito" started to play, I heard people woo with delight. I wasn't a fan of the song, but how nice it would be to go down there and drink and dance and maybe meet a cute guy and make out with him.

Ah, being alive. That would be nice. But I was too scared to go down into the streets alone. It seemed so dark and, obviously, foreign, and I was so tired from traveling. There was no way I could exercise good judgment with such a head fog. But I could totally fantasize about being there, comfortably, in a perfect world cushioned with safety and sweetness like a plump Gusher.

Was the music coming from a club? I pondered, rolling my head around the pillow. No, it sounded too loud. Almost as if there were loudspeakers in the streets. It made me think of Puerto Rico, one of the many trips I took while working remotely during my last year with Kyle, when he was distant toward me and I was pouting over our continually delayed engagement. Me and my friend Krystal visited a square exploding with nightlife. We marveled at all the dancing that spilled from the clubs into the streets. People were dancing salsa in the hot sticky air. There was such vibrancy to it.

I was determined it must be something similar. I imagined a crowd of people salsaing or - perhaps not salsa- but definitely *dancing* in the cobblestone streets. I hoped this was not a one-off event. I wanted to experience it. I listened to the music and jovial voices, including occasional woos, until I began drifting into sleep.

I woke up a few times, still hearing music, and looked at the open doors of my balcony.
Maybe I should shut them, just in case. I shrugged it off. I woke up in the middle of the night to a quiet air. No more music but more bed squeaking from above and the sound of a woman achieving orgasm.

☺

    I woke still exhausted from the journey through the sky, but with an excited mind. I turned to find Amelia snuggled next to me. Her long locks of ear hair were billowing over my right arm.

    "Amelia! Good morning!"

    She raised her head and began wagging her tail so hard that I could hear it hitting the blanket; the usual morning routine.

    "Let's go explore!"

    I scooped her off the bed and put her on the ground.

    I checked the weather. 68 degrees. Amazing. What a contrast to the 10 to 20 degrees in Vermont.

    I threw on some black cotton leggings along with flip flops and a light jean jacket over my black sleep-tee, plus a pair of cat-eye sunglasses. I hooked Amelia's leash onto her collar and took out just a few euros and slipped them into my pocket. I didn't know how safe it was out there yet. I decided it best to be cautious, especially given those blog reviews. Sure, they were probably written by jerks, but I was all alone. Last thing I wanted was to become the victim of a crime in another country; it's been rough enough trying to deal with the aftermath of victimhood in my own.

    I locked my apartment. The hallway was a pleasant surprise. Like every place you first see when it's dark and extra new, it looked much less scary in the light. Rays of sun were pouring in through some of the cement holes. Some kind of chicken wire was threaded through the holes, and through them I could see patios on the buildings next door. Kids' toys were strewn about and a balloon was tied to a bike.

    I led Amelia down the stairs to the door. I grabbed the designated key and it fit into the hole but it didn't seem to lock. I tried again. It made a clicking sound, but when I turned the handle, it was clearly unlocked.

    Hmm. At a certain point, I decided it was best to just pretend I had locked it than to draw too much attention. Besides, I could feel eyes peering at me through blankets hanging from the building just down the alley.

I didn't like how tight the alley felt, narrow, secluded. Was I under-reacting or over-reacting?

As soon as I hit the street, it was clear that flip flops were not the way to go. Everyone was dressed as if it was the dead of winter in Manhattan. Scarves and jackets and definitely no open toe shoes. A group of old men wearing newsboy hats stood next to a Sicilia Journal newsstand and looked at me - like something out of a movie - stared at me. I walked by them and kept walking. I knew there was water if I kept going, if I'd read my map properly. I walked under balconies draped with white cloths and shirts and sheets and white blankets and clothes. By the water, I passed a pond with turtles. I took pictures of it, of all of it. I figured I'd add it to my Insta story when I got back inside.

I walked up to a marina by a turquoise sea, the kind of picturesque scene I saw when Googling images of Sicily, of Palermo. Fishermen were slicing fish open for passersby. Fresh, right off the water. I marveled at it but only slightly. I remembered coming down off acid by Big Sur once, years ago with friends and how seeing a real fisherman hop out of a boat from the sea and then gut a fish open for us was such a rarity. So special. Now that I was alone, seeing stuff like that, I just felt number and weirdly on guard. I couldn't see the world like it was full of sapphires. I saw the world like it was full of shark fins, one hand obsessively reaching for my apartment key in my back left pants pocket.

I walked by a cannoli shop and got shy. I wanted to go in and order something. My stomach was growling but I was too afraid to speak. Everyone looked so intimidating. I was already regretting coming here alone. I hadn't yet said one word aloud except to Amelia. And that was just her name.

I knew I should be venturing into new and uncomfortable territory more easily, that it would be good for me. Yet, I fell back on good old English stuff instead. What was comfortable. I logged onto the ex-patriot subpage, as David suggested, and put up a message.

"Hi all, my first day in Palermo! I'm here for two months, visiting from the United States and would love to learn more about the area and make some friends!"

A few people wrote to me. Shocker: they were all men. A few were older, much older. Others were around my age. I responded to those who I would consider fucking if I thought we hit it off right, just in case that's what they were expecting. I assumed that's what they would be expecting based on the penis to vagina ratio of who was interested in "showing me around."

"I'm not gonna fuck any Mafia guys," I messaged one of my friends jokingly, mimicking David's remark from his bedroom where I hoped my butterfly clip still rested, still fluttered a part of him. Although, it wasn't *all* a joke. A part of me was worried I wouldn't be able to tell who was in the mob or not. It wasn't a huge concern, but it still looked like the Mafia was pretty active in Sicily. I even downloaded a "No Pizzo" map, for businesses who claim they don't pay the mob protection money.

"Would love to show you around," one dude named Ted wrote, accompanied by a winky face emoji. He had dark hair and dark eyes but also looked like he could be related to me. He was also tall, thin and looked kind of like a type I am often drawn to.

The wink conjured up fuck boy energy, player energy.

"Do you know what the best taxi app is here?" I asked him after some small talk.

"No, there is none."

Can't be.

"Let me drive you around," he said.

Ooh boy. A stranger asking me to get in a car.

"Maybe we can meet sometime for a drink instead."

I could meet him sometime, I thought. Or, nah. He would probably try to have sex with me. I put the idea on the backburner for the moment. Having to think about such a dilemma overwhelmed me; I was no longer physically suited for flings, I told myself.

I thought back to a friend who told me, "You're going to be fucking so many hot guys on your trip! Rebound time in Europe!"

But she also always forgot that I no longer had nipples, just gashes. In fact, she often forgot I had cancer at all. I always avoided the topic or the stigma.

Another man named Otto messaged me. He had a calmer energy. He said he was from Germany and offered to meet up as well. He was tall and relatively thin, with black hair kissed by gray streaks. He had a gentler energy about him already; at least less winky-face emojis.

I asked him about the Taxi app. I wanted the ability to go out late at night and be able to get home safely.

"No. lol we are basically in Africa," he said. "I just walk. Sometimes bus. The buses are unreliable though."

I frowned. I would have also assumed that Africa would have taxi apps. I was very confused by all of this. Was I just being an ignorant American who thought the rest of the world operated like America? Maybe! I thought back to when I went to undergrad in Montreal. Yeah, things were way different there and also confusing for me, a then-teen but I think they have Lyft and Uber there now.

I opened my Lyft and it said no cars available in this area. I opened up Uber and got the same message. I Googled Lyft and Uber in Sicily and got very similar answers to the questions I had in David's bedroom.

"There are some taxis here but not many," one person wrote.

I opened up my Google play on my phone and searched around for taxi apps. Okay this one *seems* like it could work here.

I downloaded it. It did not.

Well, one thing that has to be here is Tinder, I figured. Then, I downloaded Tinder for the first time since 2016, a little before Kyle and I began dating. Actually, I'm not even sure I had the app on my phone when we met. I think I was disturbed by the prospect of having Tinder in the small state of Vermont. When I'd flip through dudes, I'd come across former classmates, coworkers, the people that served me food at restaurants. It was like trying to pick up at a family reunion. Everyone looked familiar and if I wanted to fuck them, I probably would have already.

I was ready to see what kind of guys were in Sicily. Dark hair, dark eyes, lots of scenic backdrops. Crystal green water cascading behind cliffs and palm trees. Many of the men were in speedos. I matched with one man who looked like the Siclian equivalent of a scene kid from a few years earlier, quite a few years earlier. He could be interesting I thought, as I checked him out in his black jeans and black shirt with an Italian phrase on it. I was much more attracted to his style than any man wearing a speedo, despite him being less conventionally attractive. I liked not seeing his penis bundled up in a piece of fabric.

Gina, I told myself. Don't be so judgemental. You're in a different country. Open up your horizons.

Okay, fine. I swiped right on some speedo dudes too.

Soon messages from matches began flooding in.

Heart emojis. Heart eyes emojis. Cat heart emojis. I had never received so many heart emojis from men in my life at one time. While I had been warned that Italian men had a reputation for being aggressive, they seemed more like lovesick 12-year-old girls at this point.

"Ciao Gina, piacere," says Fabrizio. "Bellisima!" heart emoji face.

"Ciao Gina, Bella," says Luca. "Bella!!!"

He sent 30 heart emojis.

I recoiled.

"Ehhhhhhyyy," says Gaetano, the scene looking guy. I chose to talk to him for a bit until I got Tinder fatigue.

"Do you have WhatsApp?" I knew I was lazy about checking my Tinder and had been told everyone used WhatsApp in Europe.

"Yes, who doesn't?"

Uh, most of my friends in America, I wanted to say. And me, up until a few days ago.

I gave him my WhatsApp number and I received a message from him: a winky face.

⇨

A day and a half, and many heart emojis later, I decided to try to talk to somebody in person for the first time since the lady and child left me in the place. It must be done. My stomach was rumbling and I knew there was awesome food all around this island. I realized it had been quite some time since I'd said anything aloud to *anyone* except to Amelia. I knew most places allowed dogs, but I was feeling so shy. How would I ask if it was okay? What if I fucked up? What if I couldn't read body language? Maybe best to leave her the first time.

I put Amelia in the bedroom and put her water bowl on the floor and shut the bedroom door. She looked at me with concerned big eyes indicating the brink of a fit. I heard her crying as I locked the front door of the apartment.

"I'll be back, puppy pie," I told her in a high-pitched voice.

I walked out the alley and turned right on the cobblestone road and into the Saturday sun. This time I had sneakers on and a jacket over my outfit and nobody even batted an eye at me. I was dressed in all black, which seemed to mirror the style, luckily one I wore on a regular basis.

One store front had pastries facing the street. Works for me.

"Ciao," I said with a smile.

"Ciao," said a tan guy in his mid-twenties with big brown eyes and dark features.

"Como stai?" I said in a very American accent.

"Bene, bene."

I hesitated on what to say next as my heart rate increased.

"Bene," I parroted before letting out an exasperated, "Um."

I pointed to a cannolo.

"Voglio… cannolo. Um pera favora."

Stop mixing it up with Spanish, I told myself.

"Et un caffè. Un cappuccino. Grazie."

He told me to sit down. I did.

I took out my phone and stared at it until he brought me my caffeine and cannolo.

"Th- Grazie bene."

I looked at the pastry. The hard tubular shell was painted with sugar like snow and crammed with ricotta cheese. A bulbous candy cherry and a strip of candy lime stared at me from one of its open sides.

I bit into it. Okay, damn. This tasted better than any other cannolo I'd had in my life. Unlike the stale shells I was used to as a kid on Long Island, it felt soft and fresh and flaky. And the cannoli cream wasn't over-sweetened. It reminded me of when my mom was making it fresh at home. I'd lick up the cannoli cream out of a bowl and while it didn't taste like candy - it was more savory than sweet in many ways - there was something indescribably good about it.

Once I devoured it, I sipped on my cappuccino and stared at my phone. I looked at photos of Amelia and her brothers from Rebecca's house. All three dogs were running around over fallen leaves: pink, red, and yellow. Amelia was chasing after the boys: one black with brown trimming and the other tri-color. Amelia was the tiniest. I smiled, looking at the furballs. I wanted to go online but couldn't. I didn't have an international phone plan. I had set up with my provider that if I did go off airplane mode and made a call off wifi, that it would cost 10 bucks per day. That would be for emergencies. Most cafes would have wifi I figured and hell, less service might get me to actually vacation and relax and not be so fucking tethered to my goddamn phone. Only for emergencies will I use it off wifi. Most cafes have wifi all over the world, I thought. This place did not appear to have wifi. I didn't see anyone at the cafe using their laptops. Everyone was just talking, socializing, enjoying what they were eating and drinking, enjoying the landscape around them. *That* indeed felt foreign.

I waited for the check. It never came. Eventually I stood up and said "Quanto costo?"

"It's okay," he said.

He motioned his hand at me to sit and relax. But I have nothing to do and nobody to talk to, I wanted to say. I don't even have wifi. I smiled and continued staring at my phone, flipping through photos from earlier that year. Selfies of me on the couch during days when Kyle was playing video games, photos of me with grad school classmates out at a bar, pictures of me and Krystal out in Puerto Rico. I am smiling and the sweat on my forehead makes me look radiant but I remember feeling particularly ugly and fat that night. How pictures distort and hide such feelings. How looking at photos brings me back to reality instead of just obsessing in my head. Oh, I'll still be obsessing but at least I can feel like I'm in the same space as the flowers and palm trees around me instead of some sort of limbo.

I should be doing something. I should be productive. I should be writing. But before all that, I should be exploring, not just sitting here. I stewed.

Eventually, I got up and again said, "Quatro costa?"

Is it contro or costa or is that even the right word at all? I was nervous he would tell me to sit down again but he did not.

"Tre, per favore."

"Tre euro," I took some coins out of my pocket. I handed him a 2 euro and 1 euro coin.

Not bad for the best cannolo of my life.

I then wandered to the grocery store where I marveled at the prices of fucking Sicilian wine. Still feeling an undercurrent of melancholy that it sucked doing this trip solo. I was privileged, yes, but lonely. I love shopping with other people. I reminisced about grocery shopping with Kyle.

God, it was so much fun. Especially at the start of our relationship. I really appreciated him at a point when I had once again grown accustomed to doing everything alone again. I remembered one of the first times we went grocery shopping. Perhaps we weren't even officially a couple yet. I'm sure I reveled in the moment because it felt very couple-like. Nearly alone in the cookie aisle, minus one middle aged woman maybe 20 feet away, Kyle began dancing comically to George Michael's "Careless Whisper" blasting from the store's overhead speaker. The lady noticed, smirked, and backed away. I began uncontrollably giggling as Kyle wiggled and writhed his body to the saxophone sound like a snake or a penguin. I was laughing so hard that day. I felt joy. I felt alive.

    I used to go to Walmart with my roommate and longtime friend Chinga. We'd get really high and wander over to the superstore, which was next door to our self-proclaimed "luxury" apartment complex. Sometimes we'd see juggalos with knives, other times we'd see arguments - a woman berating her husband over cereal, for instance. We'd gawk at cheesy t-shirts and sometimes even buy them. I would be laughing. I felt joy. I felt alive.

    These platonic experiences with people I liked was at times better than sex.

    This new grocery store though, was like trying to maneuver with a new sexual partner, one you don't have natural chemistry with. How do I buy fruit? I bought fresh and local mozzarella, fresh and local pasta, tomatoes, local wine (three bottles worth), and staples. It came to 20 euros.

"Giuseppi! Perché la stufa è ancora accesa? Perché? Perché? Perché?" a woman's voice screamed as I stared at the ceiling from bed.

I immediately shifted my gaze toward the open french doors, a coral sheet waved in the light breeze where the sound was coming from.

Then, I heard a man scream, "Perché sto facendo le lasagne! Fermare! Fermare! Esci dalla cucina."

Were they for real yelling about lasagna? Was I hearing this correctly? Was it wishful thinking? Either way, it sounded like they were in an extremely heated fight.

Thus began a regular occurrence. I'd lie in bed with the balcony doors open listening to their hourly fights, sometimes recording it onto my phone, shooting at the door and its beautifully flowing fabric to accent the screaming.

I got up and wandered to the kitchen and poured a glass of the limoncello on top of the fridge. I wanted to go to the bars but was scared to go alone. I didn't realize I would be so scared. I guess I didn't give that aspect much foresight. I would have been scared to go to bars regardless of where I was, but the language and cultural barriers made me freeze up even more.

I'll just drink here alone instead, I figured. I have enough booze already.

After two small shots of the limoncello, I was feeling warm in the stomach. And a little bit giggly. I wrote on the kitchen blackboard "Note to self: Try not to fuck anyone in the Mafia." Then I laughed at my own joke and wished someone else, anyone, was there to witness my comical genius.

I took the bottle off the top of the fridge and took a swig straight from it. No time for cups. I jumped into the shower and wrapped the curtain around me and got ready for a good two minutes of hot water.

I stood staring at the faucets like I was looking at a calculus equation. Then I hopped out. Okay, I will wet my hair first and then put the shampoo in and then start the water. I did that and got back in. The hot water felt so comforting on my head and slimy back as the shampoo ran down it. I rolled my neck around, letting the pressure of the hot water massage me. Ahh, warmth, so good, but hard to enjoy when you know it's going to abruptly end. And… water is gone. No time for conditioner. Just enough time to wash out the shampoo.

I shut off the icy stream but it was too late. A layer of cold laminated me. I stood naked and shaking, trembling. I reached for a towel to provide a bit of warmth.

My bedroom was also cold. Hmm, I looked up at the white thing on the wall. Too bad it's only air, no heat.

As I got dressed, I looked down at the brown hairs starting to spurt up around my crotch. Really need to shave that. The shower situation isn't helping anything but still, just put some lotion on it and ..oh ya, I need to buy a razor and where would I do that? That just sounded like a whole lot more stress, struggling to communicate with my janky Italian. Maybe I should try more Duolingo.

Maybe when Krystal comes, going to a store to buy a razor would be a fun and interesting experience, but for the moment it was too stressful. Amelia stared at me with her big brown Lundehund eyes. She's gotta go out. Goddamnit, Gina put on some clothes. I was suddenly very jealous of my dog for having someone who would take care of her for her whole life.

I slipped on a heathered gray cotton thong and got mad at myself over the razor thing. What if I wanted to hook up with a guy?  Well, Gina, I told myself, if you're too depressed or whatever to figure out how to shave down there, maybe you're too depressed for sex. Dopamine and serotonin and whatnot, not something to fuck with. I knew I was depressed. Or something of that nature. It would be nice to get a therapist but that was off the table for a few months. Ugh, I totally cannot miss the deadline to apply for health insurance next year. Maybe write *that* on the chalkboard instead of the Mafia joke. Spoiler: I never did and missed the deadline.

I wished I could see my old therapist from Vermont. She gave me coping exercises for anxiety that were based in science. She even called me up after a friend of mine, who also saw her (yes, Vermont is that small), told her I helped clean up a trailer after a friend's wife fatally shot herself in it. She called and asked if I wanted to talk. I knew she couldn't say why. Probably a good idea to talk to someone after something like that. When I got to her office, I sat there and talked about what happened, all matter of factly.

"I know it should be traumatic for me, for anyone, but I guess it's not," I shrugged and added, "I feel okay. It wasn't pleasant but I'm not distraught. Thanks for checking in on me."

Wasn't pleasant but not distraught: the motto for most days. At least not outwardly distraught.

✍

    Because of the time zone, my job started at 1:30 pm instead of 7:30 am. I woke up at 7:30 local time naturally, however, and figured I'd walk around a bit and explore more of Palermo.

    I set out with Amelia down Vicolo Dei Calzonai and went to the little cafe across the street.

    "Voglio un a piccolo cassata et una cappuccino," I said, and then rolled my eyes, reminding myself to do more Duolingo that evening.

    I sat and sipped my cappuccino and took a knife to the mini cassata. The round bright green marzipan shell opened up to reveal glistening ricotta. It felt like heaven when I put it into my mouth. It melted like butter, better than butter. I couldn't believe it was less than two euros.

    I set my phone on the table along with my Kindle. I began reading more of my Spice Girl book but couldn't focus. I stared at the screen without being able to really see the words on it.

    Alright, time to go to work. I paid and headed back to my alley with Amelia wagging her tail happily in front of me. Her fawn and white fan tail swooshed left and right as she took in the smells of the street. I breathed in deep so I could too.

    I gave Amelia a treat and took a seat at the desk in my bedroom. I looked up at the white air conditioner on the wall and sighed, wishing it was a heater. Then my eyes averted to the propane heater. Maybe when Krystal comes, I told myself. A lil mishap where I set the place on fire is more manageable when I'm not solo.

    Damn, two minutes past work time. It was 1:30 pm my time. 7:30 am back in New York City. The heart of my job is at 30 Rock but my morning editor, whom I've never met in real life, communicates with me from his apartment in the Bronx. Since I've never met him, my vision of him changes daily. Sometimes he's an exhausted man with kids who he has to drive to school early before work starts each day. Other days, he's an exhausted single man dragging himself out of bed after a drunken stupor. When he's the latter, I imagine an ex-boyfriend who used to drink an entire 12-pack a night. Whatever the case, he's not exhausted-acting at all. I don't know why I picture this. He's astute and direct and funny.

    I began composing my regular morning email to him.
*Subject: Monday pitches*
*Morning! Hope you had a great weekend!*
I said nothing to him about my travels.

    I included some links to some stories that would be worth writing about in my opinion. Then I got up and tried to make some coffee on the Moka pot, just to try. I knew it might take my editor a few to get back to me. I turned on the gas stove and put the Moka on the biggest burner there is. Soon the black handle was up in flames and I was blowing it out. Goddamnit. There's a melted handle now. I touched it once it cooled down and it fell right off.

    Damnit. Now I gotta replace that.

    I'm such an idiot, I told myself, with dumb and clumsy American hands and an irrational American brain. Why did you put the smallest device in this apartment, which has a meltable attachment, onto the biggest flame catching surface available? I looked at the four burners. They were four different sizes, for a reason. Why couldn't I see this a few minutes ago? Why don't I think about things that are right in front of my fucking face? God, for someone considered smart I'm a real fucking moron sometimes.

    I poured out what was left of the espresso into a cup. It looked muddy, lumpy. I went back and looked at the computer. My editor had written back. He picked one of my pitches and also told me to write some follow up stories about the Chris and Shanann Watts tragedy out of Colorado. For those who didn't have to write about this case for weeks on end and listen to hours and hours of this asshole confessing, Chris is a married man and father who murdered his pregnant wife with his bare hands and then drove his two young daughters to an oil field where he killed them, also with his stupid bare hands. Then, he hid all their bodies on the oil field, where he worked. An affair with a coworker had in part fueled the affair. I guess he wanted to start over, but you know, a wife and kids situation was in the way.  So, he murdered them all? Not the best way to start anew.

Indeed the best way to kick off spending the rest of your life behind bars. Obviously, he would be the number one suspect.

I began writing:

*Chris Watts, who last month was sentenced to spend the rest of his life behind bars for killing his pregnant wife and kids with his bare hands, is getting no shortage of attention from secret admirers.*

It was cold so I went to the closet and grabbed another long sleeve shirt. I sat down and continued working but my hands felt like icicles too. I turned the heat fan on.  It was uncomfortable and a bit hard to focus. If only it was a little warmer. Still, I could get it done.

Writing the story, I kept getting lost in Shannan Watts' face, in a picture of her that kept popping up on Google, in news stories. I thought about how much she was demonized because of her confident, go-getter attitude. I also thought about how perfect her life looked. If her husband hadn't killed her, and his affair with Nikki ended on its own or whatever, according to your average Joe, she would have had a full life. Career, nice house, children. Loving parents too.

But just like that, she's dead. Gone. Like the flip of a switch. Like a butterfly getting sucked into a car's fan. Like a bird flying through the blue sky only to smack into a sliding door.

I kept writing about Chris:

*He's been receiving plenty of mail, even love letters.*

One woman told Chris in her letter to him that she knows he is a "good guy." "I've been watching your interview and I just became attracted to you and your story (don't ask me why) lol. [..] I would really really hope that one day you and I could meet." Her letter was loaded with doodles of hearts. Another woman included a photo of herself in a bikini, telling the family annihilator that he "honestly [has] one of the kindest faces I've ever seen" and, "I don't even know you, yet I don't want you to feel alone." I rolled my eyes.

Really doesn't take much for a dude to be considered good, I told myself. Can even be a murderer. *Especially a* murderer for some.

I went on to the next heartwarming tale: How a woman named Carla Stefaniak was killed while visiting an Airbnb in Costa Rica. Before she vanished, she had told friends and family that the power in her rental was going in and out.

"It's pretty sketchy here," appeared to be her last words before her killer got her.

I sighed as I listened to the couple fighting from the direction of my balcony area again. My doors were wide open. How to know when one is being paranoid about things being "sketchy" and how to know when one's intuition is attempting to warn you about impending doom. I for sure felt like *everything* was sketchy following my 2010 attack. Couldn't walk to work without my shoulders arching up. I was on edge. I felt like my edges were literally sharp. I'd often dress frumpy, especially while alone. Didn't want it, or something like it, to happen again. Mostly because I couldn't cope with being called an idiot or a liar and all the rest again. Couldn't deal with trying to fight through another ordeal again. I got back to my day job:

*Dirty John is a riveting new Bravo show based on the true story of a successful businesswoman who joined a dating site looking for love, but instead, found a violent con artist. Debra Newell met John Meehan, who she later found out previously earned the* *nicknames "Dirty John" and "Filthy John" on an over-50 dating site. She was 59, divorced four times, and ran a prosperous interior design firm, according to the <u>Los Angeles Times</u>. Meehan seemed like the perfect match — but it soon came out that he was anything but.*

*On the dating site, Meehan framed himself as a handsome anesthesiologist who owned multiple homes, but that soon proved to not be the case. Not only was Meehan not a doctor, but he had a history of stalking, harassing, and terrorizing women. He was known to peruse dating sites like Match.com and PlentyOfFish to lure in victims. "Dirty John" was also a convicted felon with a serious drug addiction. The story is so shocking ...*

I paused to openly scoff. Again, another successful woman lured in by some gross dude. By the time I finished work, the moon was out. It was about 9:30 p.m. and the neighbors were fighting again. The woman was screaming as the man shouted back. It sounded like they were throwing plates at one another.

Buzz.

I received a Facebook message from Otto, the German guy who offered to show me around. He wanted to know how I was doing.

"I'm good, Just listening to my neighbors fight. They seem to do that every night."

"Are you sure they aren't just talking?" he responded, adding an emoji that had its tongue sticking out. "That is kind of how people just talk here."

I leaned over the balcony to look down at the dark alley below. I knew Amelia had to pee. I knew I *had* to take her outside. But it looked so dark and alien out there.

Hmm, maybe I could let her pee on the balcony area. I knew that wouldn't be right but I could wash it off. It would be better than getting approached by some of these so-called aggressive dudes on the street. Right? So far I wasn't getting approached or cat called, just stared at, but that didn't seem to be in any sexual way, just a curious way by older men who looked like weird versions of my grandfather as they stood outside a corner store holding copies of the Giornale di Sicilia newspaper.

I coaxed Amelia to the balcony by calling her name and said, "go pee."

She looked up at me with her large eyes, confused. She wagged her tail and licked my hand. She wasn't going to pee here, but I knew her well enough to know she was full of pee.

I groaned and looked beyond the patio into the darkness of night. My heart immediately started accelerating at just the thought of walking down that alley.

"Okay, baby dog." I went back inside and she followed me, wagging her tail, already knowing that I was going to take her for a walk. She began dancing as she watched me pick her leash off the counter then tried her best to contain her excitement as I latched her up.

My heart beat even faster, thinking about that alleyway. The street itself seemed fine. Just wished this piccolo slash alley wasn't so damn dark.

I walked out the double door at the bottom of the stairway and tried to shut it with the key again. It clicked but when I took the key out and tried to open it, it was clearly unlocked. Again.

I tried the other way. Still didn't work. I could hear men talking in Italian from behind me, a pseudo-apartment on the first floor which was really just a hole in cement with some tarp hung over it, the kind of image you'd see in National Geographic. Was this the sort of poverty that those snobby British bloggers were talking about? Is this normal? Is this safe?

I tried to shut the door but it would only pretend to shut. I turned the lock and it clicked but remained open. I stood under a broken streetlamp. The only illumination the dark alley came from cigarettes through the cracks of that tarp. I figured it better to fake that I locked it than to struggle as a woman alone in the dark. Sure,

I had a dog, but she was a foofy dog. Where's a good pet pit bull when you need one?

I pulled the door as tight as I could and took a deep breath, pretending I had locked it.

We walked through the dark alley. Amelia reached and tried to eat some mashed up food lodged between two rocks in the road.

"Drop it."

She listened.

The path out of the alley suddenly seemed longer than before, almost surreal, like a hallway in *Alice in Wonderland*.

When we got out, the scary tunnel seemed to turn into a sunny street. Yes, it was still dark, but there were lamp posts and life. The streets were busy, full of teens and couples in their twenties and thirties. It felt friendly, light. White Christmas lights dangled between other alleyways.

My heart rate started to slow as I walked past a couple talking in Italian. The woman had on thigh high boots and was eating a pastry as the man beside her in tight pants and a black ribbed sweater talked loudly, gesticulating with his hands.

I sat on a bench and watched people walk by. Everyone was so well dressed for a town so full of poverty. I knew from my research that the economy was bad, but nobody was dressed like slobs. Nobody was dressed like me, like us, like Americans. Us Americans love our sweatpants, even the rich ones. I know I sure as fuck do. I may not be rich, but I have a treasure chest of comfortable clothes.

I looked across the way to see a store with green and yellow signs above its window displays, which were full of bagged pasta and olive oil, neatly stacked. "Punto Pizzo Free L'emporio," it said. Mafia free emporium basically. Or more accurately, protection money free establishments.

Back inside, I took off my coat and looked at myself in the mirror. I hated the extra weight that was still on my body and face. I had already forgotten the name of the antidepressants I blamed for this, somehow. Why can't I remember their name? Why can't I even remember the name of my rapist from 2010 without looking at the order of protection? You would think one would remember. Why can't I remember things that are supposed to be important but can remember the shape of a .wav file from 1996?

A little chilly, I put on the tiny fan heater, huddled up to it, and flipped through Tinder.

What's the point of this? I asked myself. Even if I do connect with someone well enough that I will want to fuck them, will I be able to effectively communicate with them enough to explain my cancer issue? The scars? I hadn't even hooked up with random *Americans* post-cancer, just two dudes who already knew my situation so I didn't need to spell it out for them. Plus, they already *liked* me, like as a person. How would people respond? I didn't know. When is the appropriate time to tell a man you don't really have tits? First date? Before sex? Over text? Before meeting? How would I tell an Italian? What if they don't understand and they take off my shirt and get angry at me, feeling I had somehow deceived them. Or what if they are disgusted and trying to be polite yet I'm unable to tell due to the cultural differences.

I began receiving some Whatsapp messages from Gaetano.

"What kind sex u like," with a wink face, heart emoji.

Straight to the point, eh?

"It depends," I said, then added, "on the person."

"I like sex on first date."

I sighed. I told him that it depends, and that I didn't want to meet up with that expectation.

Then he sent a voice message, "For me, I like violent sex. I like it that way."

I sighed again. I was certain he meant rough and not violent but, it made my heart batter. I wouldn't know what to do if the date went wrong and my assessment about that was wrong. It was difficult enough to know what to do when dates went wrong in America. I can barely understand the subtleties of American dudes, this is a whole new ballgame.

I drank more wine. Then Krystal called me.

"I know this is crazy but do you want to take a little side trip to Tunisia while I'm there? It's just a hop, skip and a jump away."

I looked it up, only a 45 minute, cheap flight.

"There's a travel advisory for Americans," I said.

"For what reason?"

"There was a mass shooting there in 2015," I said after skimming the article.

"I mean we are used to those here."

I laughed. "Yeah, we're used to mass shootings every other week. We should be fine."

I looked at the map. It was close to Algeria, where the guy who raped me is from originally. Really, he was just a Brooklyn boy: a wannabe actor and all. It's okay. You have to overcome it, I told myself. Besides, plenty of Americans did horrible stuff to me and people I've loved yet I'm not afraid of Americans. Well, maybe a little.

## Krystal

There's something about such a perfect friend that makes me want to turn away. Krystal is so attentive that if I tell her a story or text her something she will make sure to thoughtfully address every single word I utter or send. I'm used to loving my friends but also occasionally getting irritated by them when they interrupt or say something well-meaning but thoughtless, often about something like cancer.

But, Krystal, well, she never does that.

I, on the other hand, wouldn't even let my brain consider her arrival until hours before she came. It was just too much work. I had already put in so much just getting to Sicily. I knew it shouldn't feel like work. This was an exciting thing, all of it was. But I felt so tired. I was drained from everything, from life. And while I yearned for human connection, how nice it would be to have another body in my bed, I was definitely dreading being led away from my stewing and rumination. I wanted time to explore my renewed passion for swimming around in unhealthy thoughts, putting on headphones and staring into space, obsessing about all my mistakes, my flaws, what I could do to be better, what I should have done better in 2004, 2012, 2014, how if only I did such and such in 2015 maybe I wouldn't be the way I am now. Maybe I would be married and Kyle and I would be happy.

No. Push away that thought. If he didn't like me as I was, and yes, I made mistakes, but if he wouldn't accept that I'd owned those mistakes, gone to therapy, and put meaningful work toward the relationship, then we weren't meant to be. God, I would have killed, absolutely killed for him, or any other ex, to authentically acknowledge their mistakes in our relationship. I'd have been over the moon if they went to therapy for themselves, for me, for us. But women, we often don't get credit for that shit. I guess we're expected to be mentally ill, expected to take care of it, sweep it under the skin, so we can take care of others around us.

"I can come and get you when you get to that intersection," I texted Krystal, while she was on the plane. I didn't want her to go into the same panic I did when I arrived; the streets could be a bit confusing. Then my mind began getting upset: I had to do it myself with no help yet I'm offering help to someone else. Why am I suddenly resenting her for getting more directions and assistance getting to the place than me? Completely silly. What is fuck is wrong with me? I have issues and need to work on them. I'll get therapy again soon. God, I wish I could just drive to see my therapist. God, I wish I had a home still. I wish I wasn't just floating around in the world with my stuff in storage. Shut up, be grateful you get to travel. Your parents never even made it overseas once. Be grateful.

I pushed these thoughts away, got a glass of water, and got back to writing about murder. I opened my email. Oh, an email from an agent that I'd queried.

*Dear Gina,*

*Thank you for submitting your work for my consideration. Unfortunately, it's not quite what I'm looking to represent at the moment, but I appreciate being given the opportunity to review. Thanks again for sending it my way, and I wish you the best.*

*All best,*
*Jonathan*

I groaned. I thought back to a professor who'd told me finding the perfect agent was like finding the perfect dating partner. I remember thinking if that were true, I was totally fucked.

I maneuvered over to Google Docs and continued writing murder smut, the only thing writing-wise I was asked to do at this point in time.

*Just weeks before he killed his pregnant wife and two young daughters with his bare hands, Chris Watts was trying to figure out how to tell his mistress that he loved her.*

*The fact that Watts Googled "when to say I love you for the first time in a new relationship" is just one of many disturbing details released amongst approximately 2,000 pages worth of documents detailing the case by the Weld County District Attorney's Office. The documents were released days after Watts was sentenced to serve the rest of his life behind bars for smothering daughters Bella, 4, and Celeste, 3 and strangling his wife Shanann, who was 15-weeks pregnant.*

*In the words of Weld County District Attorney Michael Rourke at his sentencing, Watts killed them all to seek a "fresh start." It appears that fresh start included coworker Nichol Kessinger, who he'd been having an affair within the weeks leading up to his family's murders.*

God, I was getting so sick of this fucking story. Of this man. But he was good for SEO.

Then, I got the text. It was Krystal. She'd arrived.

I still had a few hours of work left, but decided to use the time picking up Krystal as my "lunch break." I walked up the street hurriedly, Amelia in tow. I tend to be in even more of a rush while I'm working. There's this fear, this nagging voice in the back of my mind, telling me that if I don't work extra that I'll lose my job, and there's no backup plan, no parents, no spouse. I knew logically I had nothing to fear; my editors always told me I was ultra-fast and if anything told me to slow down. I'm sure the times I took breaks, and particularly the times I stood in line at takeout places and whatnot, nervously tapping my feet fearing getting in trouble, didn't even register on their radar. They probably never even noticed; still, the fear was deeply embedded in me, like infected ingrown hairs.

I got to the intersection. A group of three young adults were eating deep fried seafood from red and white striped paper plates. Shrimplike vapors plumed from beyond a shop's roof. I didn't see Krystal. I crossed the street, where the number of pedestrians swelled to the point that I worried Amelia would be trampled, so I picked her up and followed the crowd. I then turned and crossed the street again to reach the third point of the intersection. Still no sign of Krystal. It was time to turn on my international phone plan.

As soon as I did, she appeared in my sight, back across the street by the seafood smoke, waving her hand and smiling. I returned the greeting. Soon we were hugging and she was kissing Amelia's head, whence commenced tail wagging and air licking.

We walked back toward my place with Kyrstal rolling her suitcase over the grooves in the street. Vespas and miniature cars zoomed around us. The panic of losing my job pulled me from within, drawing me back to the warm glow of my computer, urging me to run to it. These feelings continued as we made our way up the building's concrete stairs.

"Wow," Krystal said, as I opened the door, "This place is cute."

I smiled. "Isn't it? I love it."

It suddenly did seem cuter. I loved it so much more now that she was there. It was as if having another human around, one I knew, specifically, lit a match to the walls revealing the reality of the place. It gave the space meaning. Still, the beam from within my computer was calling me, yelling at me, demanding I cut the cute talk and get back to work. *What if you lose your job?* It whispered, *then you won't be able to travel or even live.*

I tried to suppress the voice and showed her the balcony. When we got back inside, I looked at my laptop on the desk: The screen was black, it needed attention. I sighed. *Just a minute. Don't be rude to your friend, your very good friend.* I pointed to the big heater and said "I'm too scared to use it. It's propane. I don't want to blow us up."

"What's that?" she asked, pointing to the white rectangular object on the wall.

"I think it's the air conditioner."

"It's not a heater?"

"I don't think so. I wish it had heat. I've been trying to figure that out."

"Maybe we can figure it out together."

"Yeah, that's the one thing here I've noticed. It gets chilly. Like it's never *that* cold *outside* but there's a draft in here. I've been working with multiple layers on and this little heater," I pointed to the fan at my desk. "Let me finish up work and then we can check out the city. There's some wine on top of the fridge."

I paused before saying, "I probably should have requested today off."

"Oh, it's okay."

"I am completely losing track of what days are what. Organizing for this trip has been so overwhelming. Everything has been so overwhelming since the breakup."

I was excited to finish up work for the first time in a long time. I filed yet another story about a man who'd killed his girlfriend and stood up to stretch. I turned around to see Krystal and smiled. She was sitting on my bed with a glass of red, looking extra content and rosy-cheeked.

I changed from my tee shirt into a blouse, put on some high waisted black jeans, and grabbed a clutch. It was a Betsey Johnson clutch, a parting gift from Rebecca, purple faux leather in the shape of a unicorn, with just enough room for some cash and credit cards. It had a little loop for one's wrist to go through, so that a hand could clutch the cute unicorn. I removed my ID, debit card, and a credit card from the wallet in my big purse and moved it over to the clutch. Finally, an appropriate time to use this gift.

"Should we bring Amelia?" I asked.

"I don't see why not. You mentioned that everywhere here is pretty dog friendly. We can always just sit outside."

I stuck my hand through the loop of my clutch, then the loop of Amelia's leash, and we exited.

"Look," I told Kyrstal as I attempted to lock the main doors, "It won't work. Am I just crazy or am I just bad at this kind of stuff?"

She tried and laughed. "I can't get it either but I too am bad at this stuff."

"Okay, well as long as it's not just me."

As we walked down my little alley together, even though it was not lit at all, I felt joy. Suddenly a threatening world turned into a playground. We wandered down the narrow cobblestone alleys, illuminated by white Christmas lights overhead. We met an opening to the street, dark and gray, and spotted a restaurant slash bar with outdoor seating and heaters, surrounded by white, clear tents. It was called Cavu.

"That looks nice," I said.

"I wonder if they'll let us bring Amelia into that pseudo-outdoor area," Krystal mused.

"We can ask!"

"Buonasera," a young man, maybe in his early twenties, with rimmed glasses and a button down shirt approached us.

"Buonasera," we replied, shyly.

I paused and pointed to Amelia. "Cane okay?"

He replied in English, "Hmm let me check.." he bent his knees slightly.

"Okay," I said with a smile.

He patted Amelia on the head and cocked his head, moving his mouth in a manner indicating a no.

Then he looked at me as though I was nuts and said, "Of course it's okay!! Come on in!"

Krystal and I locked eyes and laughed.

"Amazing," she said.

We followed him to a seat within a tent next to a heater.

We looked at the menu. Everything was extremely affordable.

"Let's get a cheese plate."

Our platter was composed of two wet, gooey balls of mozzarella surrounded by triangles of cheese on top a mountain of prosciutto and other meats. The mozzarella was the best I ever had. We ordered a bottle of wine. As we ate and drank, our waiter kept bending down to talk to Amelia.

We caught up, we laughed, we talked about relationship junk. I told her about David and how into him I was, I told her about the guy who told me he wanted to have "violent sex," then I told her about Ted.

"I do *not* want to fuck this guy," I said as I got my phone out from my back pocket and opened it up, so I could show her some pics of Ted with puffed up lips and all his selfies and whatnot. "He seems nice enough, but I can just tell by all his winky faces that he's the type who wants to bang foreigners. Which, I guess, nothing wrong with that, but ew."

Warm and filled with wine and food, we left and wandered around, heading back in the general direction of my place. And there it was again. That sound. The sound of very loud music coming from *somewhere.*

"I've been hearing that, at night, from my bed."

"We should check it out."

I felt a buzz from the phone in my pocket. Oh, right, I turned on the plan today to find Krystal. Now it's on for the whole day.

"It's Ted. He wants to know what I'm up to."

I sighed.

"I guess it wouldn't hurt to tell him we're headed toward the music. Maybe he can tell us what it is."

I texted him. He explained, "It's Vucciria and I'm there. Just keep walking up Victorrio Emanuele."

We did until we saw a sea of people, mostly dressed in black, spilling out of an alley filled with street carts billowing with smoke. A few skinny cops leaned back on a "Polizia" van, smoking cigarettes and talking amongst themselves.

"What *is this?"* I asked, as we entered the corridor. It was packed with people dancing, curly black-haired girls and black-haired men grooving around vespas. A few bikes had speakers on them. Several men were crowded around those. Beyond the corridor was a very slim alley packed with even more people, with open passageways to bars overflowing with patrons holding cheap plastic cups of purple and red fluid above their heads as they attempted to maneuver the crowd. There must have been at least 250 people crammed into the alley and square. Maybe a lot more. I suck at math.

"Gina," I heard a male voice say.

There he was, Ted, right in front of me, grinning. His energy was immediately less bro-like than I feared. I felt immediate relief. He was small-boned in a way that made him feel safe. He introduced us to his two buddies, who were smiling and looking at the crowd. Ted led us all into one of the open doors to get a drink.

"Ask for a Cynar. Only two euros. Very strong. It's artichoke wine."

Shoulder to shoulder, me, Krystal, and Ted waited by the bar. I took the three euro out of my pocket and held it in my hand. I asked for the drink Ted mentioned and watched the bartender press a button on a clear jug of dark purple fluid. He handed it to me in a little plastic cup. I put down a two-euro coin and a one-euro coin as a tip.

"No," Ted snatched the one euro and put up to my face, "No tipping here."

We sat at a table in the corridor with Ted and his friends, along with another group of foreigners and a local in a fedora. People danced around us. Their jeans and black stretchy pants were up to my shoulders. I tried not to assert my American judgment of a fedora upon the dude. He seemed friendly enough but it was really hard to tell if he was the Sicilian equivalent of an incel. Among the foreigners, there was a group of people from Ukraine. One was a man who I could tell was very attracted to me because he kept staring until his girlfriend, who was universally beautiful, hit him and ran off. He then tried to talk to me.

Love, it's so beautiful, I thought sarcastically as I drank my very strong artichoke wine until the dangling Christmas lights around me blurred.

I woke with a headache and dry mouth. Classic.

Amelia was stretched out in a sploot between Krystal and me in my bed. We had left the balcony doors open all night and the Saturday sunlight spilled in, cascading a rectangle on the floor, revealing some kind of food stain on my black high-waisted jeans, which had been strewn across the ground when we got home last night.

I recalled our late-night chatter. We got back and were giggling, debating the meaning of a fedora in Sicily. We were laughing about the Ukranian guy and came to the conclusion that Ted was nice enough. Maybe he was a player, based upon - oh yes, he was talking about how much he loved foreign girls and oh yes he did say he had a son with a girl from Romania, and I mentioned how I dated too many guys who liked Eastern European girls in the past - but, he was helpful and friendly enough. Just don't sleep with him, that was the consensus.

Besides, Ted had even offered to drive us to the airport during our impending Tunisia trip which was just hours away. I remembered giving him Krystal's cell phone number, so he could text her while my phone was off wifi. I turned to look for my phone, which I had conveniently placed on the wall ledge on my side of the bed, even when drunk. It was 10:10.

I curled over to look at Krystal, still sound asleep with her ear buds in. She always slept with earbuds and always listened to audiobooks of *Harry Potter* as she dreamed.

I got out of bed and put a sweater over my tee shirt and cold, bare arms. I walked into the kitchen, got a glass of water, took two Tylenol from the bottle on the counter, guzzled it all down, and sat at the kitchen table. The little window above had chicken wire around it and concrete was pouring in light, exposing a layer of dust on the kitchen table. The whole scene encapsulated my concept of a hangover.

I needed caffeine. I was sure Amelia needed to go out too. I went to the bed to scoop her up. She was still lazily curled up next to Krystal, as if she'd been out drinking too. I went to get my ID and cards out of my clutch and- oh no where did I put it!?

Didn't see it in the bedroom. I went back out to the kitchen. Hmm. I looked at the floor. I searched my jacket. Oh dear fuck, no, I told myself. Was it snatched??

I googled purse snatchings in Palermo.

"I have been to Italy several times and speak Italian," one poster on a message board stated. "I am used to being very careful of purse snatchers and pickpockets. However, the tour books I have been reading about Palermo are starting to worry me. I will be with my husband (who is quite tall and in good shape), but I keep reading things about not walking at night and saying to take a taxi after dark, etc. I am getting a bit concerned because we are used to walking almost everywhere."

Then I found another.

"We were only there for 2 hours and her purse was snatched," the post read. "We didn't think it would happen to us. We pay attention - look around, etc. My friend had a small wristlet purse. It happened so fast - probably 30 seconds. A guy came out of nowhere and pushed my friend down on the ground. Then a second guy rushed in and grabbed her purse while I was screaming at the guy."

Wait, that post is 13 years old, I realized. I found another Google hit with no date on it. "Sicily gets a bad rap," the blog said. "The island of five million inhabitants is usually mentioned in the same breath as crime, Cosa Nostra, or Corleone. But that's unfair. As a woman who has lived and traveled solo there for extended periods of time, I'd like to offer a few alternative images: warm hospitality, old-world courtesy, natural beauty, magnificent architecture, amazing festivals, vibrant cuisine."

It went on to say, "Well, okay, there was a brief encounter with Mafia-connected *scippatori* (purse-snatchers) in Palermo on my first visit there, as well as a gun battle in front of my apartment. But that was 1991, and Sicily is changing."

Alright, I thought, so that's maybe not a thing anymore. I continued reading.

"After the murders of prominent anti-Mafia officials in the 1980s and early 1990s, the Italian government cracked down on the Mafia, with considerable success. Whereas most Sicilians wouldn't even admit there was such a thing as the Mafia 15 years ago, ordinary citizens are now vocal in fighting it. In Ragusa, the gentle Baroque town in southeast Sicily where I've been living off and on since 2002, posters all over town proclaim, "*La fine della Mafia siamo noi*" (We are the end of the Mafia)."

But, I told myself, it's likely my purse was lost and swooped up. I probably held it pretty loosely and was getting kinda loose with the alcohol, and there were so many people at Vucciria. But wait, I don't recall even having it there. Hmm. Maybe I dropped it. Well, certainly if I did, the cash and cards were gone. God, why didn't I disperse some of my cash into my pockets? I just couldn't recall when it vanished. I sat in my desk chair and glared at my laptop. If only I had taken the day off work like a non-workaholic, then maybe I wouldn't have been as tired. I could have been a little less tired and a little less spacy and would've kept better track of my purse. And maybe I shouldn't have brought my dog out either. I began debating if I was even fit to be a dog mom. Why did I get a dog when I was struggling to take care of myself first?

*She wants to go out, and I have to do it*. I sighed. I found her leash on the ground and put it on her as Krystal began rustling awake.

"Good morning," she said with a squinty smile as she stretched out her arms, the sun shining on her blonde hair.

"Heyyy," I said. "Morning."

"Going for a walk?"

"Yeah, wanna come?" I asked. "I think I either misplaced or lost my purse."

I thought back to when Rebecca gave it to me. I thought back to envisioning myself wearing it on a night out here and sending Rebecca a picture with it to thank her. *Too overwhelmed to even take a pic*, I scolded myself.

"Oh no!!!" she said, *very* sympathetically. Sometimes Krystal was so emphatic and sweet it made me uncomfortable. It just wasn't something I'd been accustomed to most of my life, and instead of wrapping myself in the comfort of it like a blanket, I distrusted and saw it as abrasive.

"It's okay," I shrugged. "No use in me getting too upset. Won't change anything."

"Maybe you lost it while we were walking around," she offered.

"Yeah," I said. "In that case, its contents are probably gone, but who knows if someone returned it to a business or something."

"Let's retrace our footsteps from last night."

I smiled and nodded. It was something my mother would have said. She was always so good at finding lost items. She had a math mind, a logical mind, something that was not passed on to her daughter.

We intended on getting some caffeine to go but the people working at the cafe across the street from my place looked at us like we were absolutely nuts, so we figured why not just sit and have a cappuccino first. It wasn't like the purse was going anywhere, and the cafe didn't have to-go containers anyway. Or take-away containers, as they say in Europe.

After sucking down our caffeine, we headed back down the cobblestone alleyways toward Cavu. Vespas passed around us constantly like hornets. When we got to the open area with the Christmas lights, now turned off in the daylight, I started searching.

In the daylight, I noticed two large trash barrels in the square. If I was to have found a purse, and I was looking for a quick buck, I'd rip out the cash, take the cards and then dump the purse in the trash. I looked into both trash bins. Just glass beer bottles and half eaten pastries and tissues and a half sandwich.

A man was standing outside a fancy looking restaurant overlooking the square, smiling at us. I figured it was worth a shot to ask him.

"Anyone leave a purse here?" I pointed to the crossbody purse that Krystal was wearing.

"You give hug, I answer."

I looked at Krystal and rolled my eyes. It was humiliating. Then he put his arms around both of us and told us to hold on. He went inside.

"What is going on?" I mumbled to Krystal.

The man walked back out and pointed to a bar across the street. A woman was standing outside the bar.

"I think they have it."

"Oh?" I felt fluttery!

We walked over to the spot.

"Gina!" she said.

"Oh! Yes, I mean si!"

"Your purse. We have."

A man walked over from the bar inside the establishment and said, "We ah message you on Facebook. You don't see?"

"Oh no! I did not. I, wow, thank you so much!!! Grazie"

He went back to the bar and bent over slightly, grabbing something from under the register and there it was: my unicorn cat.

"Grazie millie!! Grazie millie," I said, feeling myself deflate with relief.

"We should get a drink here," Krystal mumbled to me, smiling.

"Yes," I said. "Of course."

I wanted to leave an extra big tip.

We sat down. Ordered some drinks.

I unzipped the purse. My cards were inside, as was my money!

"Look, it's all there, all of it, even the cash."

"Wow! That's impressive."

I thought back to when I was younger and I pocketed 40 bucks from a wallet I found on the ground. I did return it though. Wow, these so-called poverty-stricken people had better morals than Americans, than me.

I couldn't wait to tell David how these "poor people" behaved, "Man fuck that British bitch," I would message him.

"That was awkward, the hugging guy," I mumbled.

"I know, I never know what to do in those situations. Where's the line between culture and misogyny?"

I heard a ding. It was Krystal's cell. I suddenly felt like this world, which was once scary and unknown, was now not. It now felt comfortable, like a towel that's been in a family closet for years.

"It's Ted," she said. "He wants to know what airline we are using."

"TunisAir. 1:15 p.m."

"Thanks." She texted him back.

"Wow, I can't believe we are going to be in Africa in a few hours."

"Oh my god, I know!"

Ding.

It was Ted again, Krystal explained, showing me the text on her phone while I took a sip of wine.

"Prepare for delays. Lol ;) "

"Uh oh," I said. "Gulp."

"Oh no, maybe they are notorious for delays? Well, we aren't in a rush are we?" Krystal said sipping her wine.

"Cheers to that," I clanked her glass with mine.

"Damn that was weird about the guy in the square," she whispered. "I never know what to do in those kinds of situations."

"Same," I said, "Especially in a foreign country. It's like a struggle within me between being anti-patriarchy versus being polite in another place."

"Right!"

We finished up and I left a 40-euro tip, and stuck a candle on top of it, to say thanks. Then we walked back toward my place and went down another little side street full of pizza restaurants. We went to a place Ted suggested. Each pizza, the whole pizza, was 3 euros. We ordered two pizzas. I ordered an anchovy pizza and Krystal selected one with piles of meat upon it, thinly sliced.

On the morning of the Tunis trip, Krystal and I woke to the sounds of explosions outside.

My mind immediately thought of car bombs. I thought back to the research I did on the trip, how in the 1990s the headlines read "Palermo just like Beirut" after a series of Mafia-orchestrated car bombs.

I texted both Ted and Otto.

"I didn't hear it," Otto said. "Probably fireworks."

"Well," I told Krystal. "I guess if they aren't concerned, then whatever."

"Yeah, it's like being on an airplane; always look to the flight attendants to see if they are worried."

Ted even drove us to the dog sitter's house, whom I'd hired on Rover. En route we passed some castley-looking homes surrounded by concrete walls like fortresses or compounds. The dog sitter's home was located in such a compound. We got to the gate and buzzed. They opened the wire gates and we drove through a bright colored yard full of kittens, dogs, and lemon trees.

We got out of the car and Ted yelled, "Bonjourno!" to a woman, perhaps in her 40s, walking out of the house wearing black jeans, a black sweater, and patent leather boots. A child, maybe 12 or 13, came out wearing a multicolored sweater with jeans and holding a shitz-zu.

I waved and smiled.

"Adianmo dentro!" the mother exclaimed.

"She say to come inside," Ted told me.

"See, I can be your translator," he said, massaging my forearm slightly and briefly. I admit, in the moment it felt nice and safe. Maybe I should hook up with him, I thought. I'd have a built-in tour guide, a translator, and a man with a car. Who cares if he's not perfect for you? He's an attractive man; many women would call me crazy for not just accepting this easy key.

Amelia cried as we left. When we got back on the road, Ted said "I think we have more than enough time to take you two to Monreale."

I looked at my phone. It was 11:30am. "Are you sure?" I asked from the backseat, nervously. Being the kind of person who *needs* to get to the airport early, I seriously questioned if we had time. Plus, Italians were rumored to be notoriously late.

"Yes, your flight will be late."

"Let me check," Krystal said, sitting shotgun. We drove past gray and pink concrete walls, some with lemon trees and tropical flowers peeking from the tops. Ted began driving uphill on a windy road. The sun passed through the back window and warmed my right cheek.

"Ahh looks like our flight *is* delayed, two hours!"

"Told ya," Ted gloated from the driver's seat.

"Oh," I conceded, "I guess we're not in a rush."

"Nope," Krystal confirmed. "We can explore here and then take it easy and explore Tunisia tonight!"

The car climbed a steep cliff, mountain peaks visible to our left. Giant purple flowers peeked through wire gates which protected houses from the narrow road. We took a few sharp turns and came to a town center. Ted parked his little car into a tight spot and led us to a busy cafe swarming with people, mostly old men with gray hair and glasses wearing tan coats.

Once we managed to get to the counter, I ordered a cappuccino.

"Due euro cinquanta," the cashier told me.

"No. Dalle il prezzo reale! Non il prezzo turistico!" Ted yelled.

"Okay, okay," the man said. "Un euro cinquanta"

I took a euro out of my purse and put it on the counter.

"He was trying to rip you off," Ted told me. "See, stick with me and I'll protect you."

He winked.

He hovered over the worker like a hawk as Krystal made her order, then got a cannolo and espresso for himself, aggressively glaring at the cashier the whole time.

We sat at a round table outside. Mopeds and vespas drove by buzzing like hornets.

"Don't let anyone rip you off in Tunis," Ted warned. Sugary flakes fell from his pastry. "Trust me, they will try. You have to negotiate with the taxi drivers before you get into the car."

The flight took off late but was remarkably short. We touched down in Tunis within 40 minutes.

As soon as we entered the airport, full of white walls and Arabic text, I knew I was out of my element. My heart began to pound, trying to determine how to maneuver a new place that was likely even more different from my bubble than Italy, which had been challenging enough. We walked to the cab lot and a dude pointed us to a dude in a car.

I smiled at the man, then stopped and averted eye contact, too much eye contact or turning up of the lips and one may think you find them attractive; that's what life has taught me.

"Le Medina, s'il vous plait," I said as we stood on the curb holding our bags. I forgot how to say "how much?" in French, so said it in English.

"Yes yes, come in," he said, reaching for my bag. "That's good."

I held my bag tight and didn't let go. "How much?"

"Yes, get in."

Suddenly, several other male taxi drivers parked ahead and below started yelling at us.

"Get in. Get in. Get in."

Krystal and I locked eyes. I felt the urge to run.

"How much?" she asked.

"Get in," he said.

This was proving to be harder than it seemed.

Even more men started yelling for us to get in. We both shrugged and did so, reluctantly. Our eyes remained locked to each other's as the driver pulled onto a highway and began cruising past billboards printed in Arabic.

"When you leave?" the slightly rotund man asked.

"Monday."

"To airport?"

The driver pulled his phone out of his right pants pocket and, while driving, pulled up Google Translate.

He wrote something in Arabic and held the phone up between the driver's seat and passenger.

It translated to English: "Do you want me to attack you?"

A familiar feeling hit my stomach, like butterflies but the opposite. Like a galloping horse getting stuck in the mud. My mind became instantly fluttered. I looked around the car for exit options and items to fight off the driver with. Would I open the door and tumble out? Would Krystal do the same? Would we both attack him, or would we flee? Out the window were just highways and billboards. I wondered if someone saw two white girls running, would they help us or just laugh, or maybe just convince us to get back in the car with this guy.

Okay, maybe that's not what he meant.

"Bad translation," I muttered with a smile.

He typed something else in his phone and held it up.

"I miss you," it read.

I felt my face flushing. I looked at Krystal's face, typically amicable, drenched in worry.

"Bad translation," she said.

Soon he was dropping us off in front of the Medina, smiling and waving.

By the time of me writing this book, I am confident that is all it was: something lost in translation. Sure, he tried to stiff us for extra money when he dropped us off, but that seemed just dandy in comparison to what could have been.

I thought back to the night I was trapped in a car and didn't fight. I froze. I told him to let me out of the car but when he told me he would he just kept driving. I texted my friend for help. I verbally fought with my attacker that night and fought back some physically, but was scared if I tried to *really* combat him, he may hurt me. And by hurt, I mean maim or kill. What would I do if I were in that situation again? Probably try something different, I guess.

It was already quite dark when we walked into Medina. Krystal had booked a room at La Chambre Bleue, a bed and breakfast that boasted crossed vaults and columns remaining from the XIVth century. We dropped off our bags in the large, marble and stone filled room and wandered down white alleyways filled with hanging green vines kissed with baby blue doorways. The aesthetic was so magical I had to snap myself into the reality that we were really just in a Muslim version of Canal Street.

Walking around the market area, we drew some attention.

"You girls like Trump?" a man yelled from his shop.

Ugh. We stuck out and I didn't like it. It wasn't that I felt scary vibes perse, it was just the unknown I guess. I think I was still in fight or flight mode from the "attack" message. We stuck out and people were looking at us the same way they looked at me for wearing flip flops in Sicily.

Krystal made reservations at Dar El Jeld, a fancy restaurant in Medina also filled with mid-century pillars. To get in, we walked through a human size door hidden inside a gigantic yellow door resembling a massive Middle Eastern keyhole.

I was surprised to see they sold wine. While Tunisia is a Muslim country, alcohol is served in upscale restaurants. I skimmed an NPR article that said alcohol is a point of contention in the country as they try to decide what kind of nation to become following the revolution.

We ordered a bottle of local red and began drinking as live music played in the background. We ordered couscous, meat plates, a tagine, some dish loaded with shrimp and sardines in oil, and a custard-looking snack.

Soon, we were nearly half a bottle in. I felt warm inside.

"I can't believe that we took that trip to Monreale today and then had that weird cab experience," I exclaimed. "Like, how is this all the same day?"

"I know!" Krystal said. "Mmm, this is sooo good."

"I know," I parroted.

A man, not a waiter, perhaps a manager, who looked to be in his sixties, grabbed both our hands and led us, hand in hand in hand, to go pay. Others in the restaurant watched. Was this normal? Were they afraid we wouldn't pay?

When we got back to the hotel, I went to pee. By the toilet there was a metal hose I hadn't noticed before.

"Wow, this is like some kind of special bidet!" I began giggling trying to imagine how to use it, picturing it losing control like a snake, wiggling around and spraying the whole place floor to ceiling. David would like to know about this. *Wait. No. Do not message David about toilets again.* But the pull to do so was so there.

In bed, Krystal downloaded Tinder and began chatting with a local woman named Emine while I kept imagining myself spraying the walls with the bidet hose. I muffled my laughter through the pillow.

"We should meet up with this woman. She said she can show us around."

"You wouldn't mind me being a third wheel on your date though?"

"Are you kidding? Of course not."

"Hmm, a lesbian Tinder date in a Muslim country. Gulp."

Krystal laughed, "Yeah I asked her about that. She said we just can't make out or anything in public."

"I wonder how strict the rules are against that here."

"She said not very but it's not technically okay"

I grabbed my phone from the stone night table on my side of the bed and Googled "Tunisia" and "gay friendly."

"Both male and female same-sex sexual activity are illegal," I read the top result aloud.

Krystal giggled, "Oh boy."

"But," I read more results, "it did make the list of '5 Most Gay-Friendly Arab Countries' according to one site."

"Tunisia is the first country in the Arab world to have an LGBTQ radio station," I skimmed the article, "Whilst homosexuality is illegal in Tunisia with up to 3 years imprisonment [...], activism is so strong that there are signs this is likely to change very soon."

"I mean I'm sure they may think we are a couple or something. We only have one bed."

"I think we'll be fine," Krystal said groggily, skipping into a yawn.

I woke up to mosque chants from afar and rolled out of bed. I looked back to make sure I didn't wake Krystal. Her eyes remained closed, her headphones still tightly in her ears. I walked over to the edge of the room to look up at the ceiling, which went stories up, covered in stone. There was some wire on top of it, but through it all was a bright blue sky with just one puffy cloud quickly fluttering by.

I slipped my laptop out of my bed and put in the internet code. The wifi was slow but I managed to conduct my morning doomscrolling routine. I thought back to the last year of dating Kyle: the times that we *were* in bed together, he'd scroll through Facebook and Reddit and just about anything he could rather than look me in the panes of glass upon my face.

Soon enough, Krystal was up and stretching like a cat and we went upstairs to eat yogurt and pastries in an all-blue room.

"Can't wait to meet Emine," Krystal said of our mystery woman. "She's tall, just my type."

"But she sounds more blunt, or I suppose honest, from what you told me. Which I think will be a nice change from your ex."

"Definitely."

Krystal's ex would get jealous when Krystal was complimented. She also did not communicate, was passive aggressive, and unappreciative. To boot, she was ultra-Christian and had a lot of guilt about "sinning." She even sent a religious card to Krystal's home following their break-up, which insinuated that Krystal was going to hell for being queer.

"What time are we meeting her?"

"One p.m. at the Ancient Carthage runs. Maybe we can explore the Medina until then."

"Sounds great."

We wandered around the long stone white halls of the Medina near our temporary place. Canary yellow and bluebird blue doors, some pointed at their tops, splashed bright easter egg colors about the cobbled alleys. We walked under round archways and entered the market. Leather bags, hats, sunglasses, and rugs hung in bundles and packs.

"I can't believe we're in a market that dates back to the 13th century," Krystal almost whispered.

"I know. So crazy."

We got lost in the Medina and asked a man for directions. He instead led us up four flights to a touristy but beautiful room that went to a rooftop. The floor had the same tiles as my kitchen in Palermo, but with more blue tones. A pair of wooden canary blue shutters surrounded a window overlooking the city landscape of nearly all white buildings, like rectangular clouds. Two chairs resembling multicolored thrones for children stood beside a bed surrounded with drapery and a golden arch.

"Historic," the man said. He gestured toward the roof. There were a fair amount of people around us, and I got decent vibes from him, plus he seemed feeble. The rooftop was a tile heaven. Chunks of tiles glued to the ground, the walls - with the exception of a few chunks made of baby blue fence - and tiled archways. There were tables and chairs like an outdoor cafe. A group of four young people sat chatting amicably in Arabic. The rooftop was an explosion of colors, particularly in comparison to the sea of white squares and white domes beyond.

"Okay, now I show you to my perfume shop."

*Crap.* I reached into my pockets to see if I even had any dinari left after yesterday's dinner and drinks. There were at least a few. I began to feel my head starting to pound.

We followed him downstairs to a stand of vials filled with liquid. He tried to sell me a small bottle of a perfume made from cactus that he said smelled just like Coco Chanel.

"See?" he said. "Give me your arm."

He sprayed a bit on my left wrist, right onto my upside-down heart tattoo. I sniffed it.

"I love it!"

"Ten dinar."

"I only have eight."

It was true.

"Okay, okay okay."

"What about for the tour?"

Fuck, I thought.

I could hear Krystal shuffling her pockets behind me.

She gave him all she had, five dinar.

He didn't look too pleased. His previously smiling demeanor changed.

Krystal and I left his shop, murmuring our guilt.

"Ugh, I'm such an idiot," she said. "I should have known it wasn't a free thing."

"No, I feel the same," I said, admitting. "I'm a little hungover. Can't think straight."

"I guess we need to go to the ATM."

"Yeah."

We wandered off the Medina and into the city and found a drugstore with an ATM. We both got some dinari and I bought some Advil for my head. I tried to buy tampons, as I could feel my period coming on, but they didn't have any.

A few steps away, a closed store had a sign that said *Tampon Naoui*. I took a picture, because of the tampon element. The sign featured a cartoon caricature, possibly of a stamp, but I like to think it was of a tampon.

We went to a taxi station to find a ride to Krystal's date. As we approached the line of cabs, Krystal turned to me. "Let's try this again."

"Yeah let's hope we can do it. I'll try to work the janky tidbits of French I know, maybe?"

"Yeah Arabic and French are the top languages here, so.. Emine said the cab should only be twelve dinari and said to call her if we had trouble communicating, so we can put her on speaker."

"Oh, amazing!"

We walked up to a man, thin and gray haired, dressed in dark green felt slacks and a button up shirt.

"Bonjour," I said, trying to drape my insecurities with forced confidence. "Carthage ruins, s'il vous plaît."

He responded in Arabic, and then with, "Get in."

"How much?"

"Get in."

"Twelve dinari?" Krystal asked.

"Okay, okay," he said. "Good. Good."

As we got in the cab, I felt bubbling in my chest.

We drove through winding streets before turning into what seemed like a downtown area. It was bustling with people. A man, who appeared homeless, was sitting on the sidewalk leaning against a wall. He looked as though he was actively dying, a literal white-ish layer of film over his eyes. Our cab driver stopped at the intersection and I got a real good look at him. He made me feel sick inside with guilt. A multicolored kitten with patches of skin falling off walked near him. The eyes on the cat looked sickly, puss had gathered up in the corners of each eye and the rest of the lid was covered in crust.

I responded by taking my new perfume out of my purse and rubbing it profusely onto both my forearms. I thought about how he called it a cactus base. A cactus, a flower, same thing.

Soon we were out of the city, passing through a suburban area that reminded me more of home. But then the houses got bigger and swelled up to even bigger, to homes that looked more like mansions. Our driver pulled up to a long gate that was closed with a lock around it. I could see the ruins just over the horizon.

"I think the entrance is around the corner." Krystal handed the man twelve dinari.

"No. Venti!"

"What?" Krystal asked.

"He says twenty," I said, lowly. "Damn."

"No, we agreed.. I'll just call Emine."

"Hi there," Emine answered in a flirtatious tone, her voice low and furling like a cat.

I looked at our driver's eyes in the rearview. His brow was furrowed.

"Hi Emine," Krystal said ecstatically, "we are close, at the closed gate."

"Oh, you need to drive around the corner."

"Yes, trying to get the driver to do that. Also, we agreed to twelve but he is charging us twenty."

"Let me talk to him."

Krystal pushed the phone past the two front seats. The driver and Emine spoke in Arabic for about a minute and a half.

"Okay you should be good," Emine said.

"Okay thank you. See you in a minute."

The driver did not move forward. He did not accelerate. "No. Out."

We got out and he sped off.

"Well, that was stressful," I said, looking at the ruins in the distance. A man who'd been standing at the gate ran up to us.

"For ten dinari, I show you around."

"No, it's okay. It's okay."

We began walking ourselves around the corner. He followed behind.

"Oh my god," I whispered. "I can't wait to meet Emine. Please, let her be normal. Let her be cool."

The man behind us wandered off. We continued up to the entrance of the ruins. Krystal called Emine and told her the driver wouldn't drive any further and that we were on foot.

"I'll come meet you."

Krystal stared intently into her phone, pressing buttons. "Oh wow."

"What is it?" I looked over my shoulder.

"The difference between twelve dinari and tweny is like nothing. Twelve is like four bucks American and like twenty is like a little over seven."

"Wow, really? That's wild."

"Yeah! Why are we squabbling over a few bucks?"

"Right! I guess if they want it that bad, maybe they need it. Who cares? It's so inexpensive."

"Why is everyone so adamant about this here? I guess nobody likes to feel ripped off."

"For sure," I said, "plus everyone keeps telling us to make sure we are not."

"It's like, was I really just fighting with that man over two dollars? I'm so embarrassed!"

"Oh well, I guess next cab ride, we can just relax."

"It's so stressful to fight."

"It is. I hate it!"

We passed some flowers and arrived at another gate, this one open. A woman with dark hair and tight blue jeans stood in front.

"Krystal," she said, with a lusty looking gaze. She hugged my friend very tightly.

I started to feel this particular new world change from a strange minefield to a playground.

We paid to get into the ruins and soon enough Krystal and her date were holding hands. Emine was stroking her shoulder and back as they stood in front of a pile of rubble.

"Are you sure that this is okay?" Krystal asked.

"Yes, holding hands is fine. Kissing, not so fine."

I couldn't tell if Krystal was into it. She *seemed* into it, but is also a very polite person.

We ducked into a cave-like crevice that appeared protected from the outside world. Emime went in for a kiss. I turned away until I heard the lip and tongue smacking sounds cease.

"Oh, a bathroom," I said. "I have to pee."

"Me too," Krystal said.

We walked into a bathroom with a concrete floor and puddles everywhere. We chose stalls next to one another. I looked around for toilet paper but there was none. Just another one of those long hoses.

"Um.."

"Yeah same," Krystal laughed.

"What do we do? Try the hoses? I guess this is why the floor is so wet. No *caution, wet floor* signs here, I guess."

I turned the faucet on the hose, or at least what I thought was the faucet. Nothing came out, not a drip.

"Damn it! I can't get it to work."

"Me either."

I opened my purse with one of my hands while it hung over my shoulder hovering slightly above my leg. I continued to hover over the toilet. My upper thighs starting to go sore. I knew I didn't have any tissues but I figured I'd maybe have *something* usable.

"I uh, found a receipt I'm gonna use," I said.

"Same," I heard through the stall wall, along with crinkling.

"We gotta get some tissues for our purses."

I wanted to ask if she got a good read off Emine but I opted against it. Emine might be within earshot, and if Krystal was actually uncomfortable, she'd probably let me know by this point.

After the bathroom Emine asked if we wanted to get in her car and go for a ride.

"As long as you won't feel like I'm a third wheel," I told Kyrstal.

"No, don't be silly."

We followed Emine to her new Mercedes, black and shiny.

"I'm going to take you to Sidi Bou Said," she said. "It's beautiful, all blue and white, and it overlooks both the Mediterranean and Gulf of Tunis."

In the parking lot stood a man selling blue and white plates.

"Hmm, maybe I'll buy one," Krystal said.

Emine walked up to the man. They seemed to argue in Arabic.

"You two wait in my car." The car beeped from the alarm in her right hand. Within minutes, Emine was back at the car with the seller shouting at the door, holding two plates, half gift-wrapped.

"No," she said, turning to us. "They are trying to rip you guys off."

I felt kind of bad. I'd assumed that, yeah, he probably was, but if it was anything like the cabbie from earlier, who cares? It was a plate from Tunisia and just a few bucks extra. Still, I didn't speak. I didn't want to be rude to Emine, who was being so hospitable and who morphed this obstacle course of a world to a breeze as light as a summer day after downing a few drinks by the pool.

With the windows open and the sun soaking into my cheeks, we drove past greens until Sidi Bou Said. Narrow, winding streets were littered with orange trees. When we parked I was blown away by all the blue and white before me. It was like being inside a painting.

We walked up to Cafe des Delice, a cafe filled with outdoor seating and blue tents overlooking the Gulf of Tunis. Emine ordered a soda in Arabic for me.

"Thank you," I said, sipping through a straw at our new Tinder friend.

"Yeah, it's all a bit easy when someone can speak the language huh? You're welcome."

As we sat amongst the whites and blues of the city and the long blue sea, the scenery was so mind-blowingly gorgeous I couldn't wrap my mind around it. It was one of those images that was so pretty you felt guilty you weren't able to soak every pixel of its beauty up inside of you. I fell into the painting, so to speak, as Krystal and Emine's conversation faded to the point where I couldn't hear them.

I was abruptly pulled out of my illusion when Emine asked, "Do you ever try with women?"

Taken aback, but not shocked, I nodded. "I've tried. Sort of, a few times, but nothing too.. I don't know.."

I had only kissed other women in my twenties when heavily intoxicated.

"Maybe just not the right one," she said.

I laughed, but Krystal and I shot each other a glance, the kind indicating we were uncomfortable, but well, not that uncomfortable. Plus, I couldn't imagine what we'd do if we truly pissed this woman off and she just left us here. I'm sure we'd make it back to our bed and breakfast just fine, but it would be another obstacle course filled with Google Translate hurdles.

"Nah, I just keep going back to men. Even though they have a bad track record with me. I'm a sadist I suppose." I laughed.

"Bad track record with all of human history," Emine said. Krystal and I nodded.

After the cafe, she drove us to a fancy restaurant called The Cliff, also overlooking the sea. We got a bottle of wine and drank and ate pizza. At some point, Emine asked, "What's that on your arm?"

She was pointing to the black ink on my right forearm. Slightly warm from the pizza, I had rolled up my sleeves to half forearm, revealing the phrase "write to kill" and the barrel of an M16 etched on my skin.

I rolled it up all the way to show her.

"Bold," she said.

"It's just like, a writing symbol."

"Sure you're not a spy?" she said with a laugh.

Leaving the restaurant, we passed by some extremely well dressed folk: a woman who looked like an actress or an influencer, like Michelle Pfieffer but 19, in a pants suit and red lipstick, and men in suits. In the parking lot, all the cars were luxury cars like Emine's, new BMWs and Mercedes, even a Maserati. I thought back to the homeless people I saw on the streets earlier that day and the cat with the diseased looking eyes. Big and obvious disparity between the rich and poor here. It reminded me so much of the United States.

Emine dropped us off at a mall while she went to visit her mom. It reminded me of the University Mall in Burlington, Vermont. At least from the parking lot.

"You two shop. I'll be back in 30 minutes or less."

The inside of the mall was also very American. There were escalators and obviously lots of stores. We wandered into a few clothing shops and I scourged the racks. In one store I saw a shirt I sort of liked. Maybe I was just in a foreign country and wanted a cool souvenir. It had a pineapple or something on it. I held it up, then frowned. No, I didn't like it. In another store, I looked at some classic style tees, but they were made in China. I wanted to want something so badly but just, nothing stuck out.

I finally found a shirt I felt lukewarm about. I stood in line to buy it but Emine texted Krystal, letting her know she had arrived. Seeing as there were two people in front of me in line and the person at the register was talking with the cashier, I figured it was better to put the shirt back.

We got to Emine's car and I slipped into the backseat behind Krystal. It was dark now, but I could see from the cascading parking lot lights that she was holding a towel with something in it. She unraveled it. There were two bowls in her hands, not too different from the plate that Krystal was considering buying over at the ruins.

"One for each of you," she said, lovingly.

As Emine drove us through lamplit streets, I looked at myself in the reflection of the backseat window, wondering why I wanted to buy something so badly at the mall. I now had this bowl, a priceless token, a memory of this trip far more memorable than any shirt bought here but made in China. Still, I had a pang of regret for not buying something at the mall, like it was deeply encoded in me. Like I was a game programmed to do that.

She dropped us off at the Medina. Emine and Krystal had a swift make-out session before saying goodbye. We got back to the room and giggled.

"Do you think she stole those from her parents' house?"

The trip had been so surreal, in such a pleasant way, that I hadn't even looked up our check-in time for the next day. We were, in theory, supposed to fly out at 10 am. However, I assumed based on Ted's confidence regarding the tardiness of TunisAir, that this would likely shift to a noon flight or something. As long as I could start work by one-thirty p.m. local time.

"Oh god," I stared at my email, "It says our flight has been delayed until two p.m."

The stress and fear of losing one's job began to bubble in my stomach. Or maybe it was just cramps. I went to the bathroom to discover a small speck of blood on the inside of my thong.

"Damnit." I wasn't supposed to be having my period right now. I did, as I usually do, pack a few emergency tampons. I left the bathroom area to fish around for one in my bag.

"Just started my period," I mumbled to Krystal. "I think I only got a few tampons left. Do you happen to have any?"

"I don't. Sorry."

"Oh, it's okay!"

"We can look tomorrow. I'm sure a store will have them, or at the very least the airport."

"What should we do tomorrow? Go to the airport earlier? With our suitcases?"

"Would be cool if we could stay here an extra few hours so we can explore and leave our suitcases here. I'm gonna message our host."

As she messaged her, I composed an email to my bosses: "I was supposed to be back at my new home by Monday morning (late Sunday NYC time) but my flight is apparently delayed over twelve hours so I have to take a one-hour flight at the same time work starts and before then am stuck in Tunisia. But I will be able to work the morning until 12ish. I'm so sorry about this. Tuesday I originally requested off but because of this can totally work or just do a half day. I can also work when I land. Also, after this I'm pretty much staying put in Italy so this shouldn't happen again. Thank you and I'll keep you updated."

# Chinga

Not only was our bed and breakfast host gracious enough to let us stay until our flight, she said it was cool if I worked upstairs since the wifi was wonky in our room. She didn't even charge us extra when we offered to pay.

Surrounded in a room by bowls on the walls, baby-bird blue and white like the bowls that Emine gifted us, I opened my email. I could hear a mosque making music in the background and thought maybe if I had taken time off today, just in case, it would sound even more beautiful. But my ass never took off enough time for buffering. My editor sent me two morning stories to write up: "Miss Kentucky Busted for Allegedly Sexting Teen Student" and an update on Cyntoia Brown. Tennessee's Supreme Court seemingly decided that Brown, who was sent to prison as a teen for killing a man while she was being sex trafficked, had to serve at least 50 years before being released.

"Great news, Emine is gonna drive us to the airport" Kyrstal said, brushing her upper ear-length, wet, blonde hair. "She's gonna be over in a bit. Maybe we'll hang out in the room while you work."

"Oh, great," I said, struggling to focus. The internet was still slow. Pages were taking forever to load.

Krystal perused her phone, learning the rich history of Tunis, feeding me summaries of her discoveries.

"Really, when you think about it, their revolution was only a few years ago, 2011. Pretty interesting. Overthrowing the government always seems so foreign but we don't realize how easy it could happen in the United States too. It's all threads away, thin lines."

As the mosque music ran in the background, she noted that the population was 99.1% Muslim.

"Hmm," I said, shifting my eyes over the article on my laptop, "I wonder how religious Emine is. Or, more so, her parents. I wonder if she's out."

A Facebook message from Chinga popped up.

I knew it was around 5 in the morning where he was. Based on the typos, I assumed he'd been up all night, probably drunk.

"I'm gona paint a pic of you as a Pasta queen and a buNch of dudes in speedos putting you in pasta sauce."

"Chinga, are you high?."

"Just whiskey."

I laughed.

"What are you so intent on?" Krystal said, observing me finally focusing on the screen.

Chinga was sending pics from when we lived together with the note, "good times."

Chinga? Nostalgic? Interesting.

I laughed and said, "I think Chinga's drunk."

My worries about work fell to the wayside and I honed in on Chinga. This kind of insight was so rare with him, like shooting stars in a usually stoic black night sky, with light pollution purposely covering up any possible beauty.

"He's talking about stockings now," I mumbled.

Krystal's phone hummed so hard it moved across the table. She picked it up.

"She's here. Can't wait to hear more about this," she said with a giggle.

"Stockings just look so professional and good," Chinga wrote. "I remember when we were roomies you had them on once, I thought they looked so hip on you. We took Molly that night and I wanted to touch them so bad but didn't want to make things awkward. I was trying to find a way, maybe offer you a massage or something."

I stared ahead at one of the bowls hanging on the wall and noticed a chip in it. I sighed, scrambling over how to respond. If I reacted with flirtation, it may scare him away. If I react too stoically, it may insult him.

"I think you know I would have been fine with that," I wrote. "Plus we were on molly."

"Yeah true lol."

I thought about the times we did molly together. There were only a few. Once on Christmas eve, but I was wearing jeans, and a tshirt with a festive cat we'd found together at Walmart. We went bar hopping with a dude who lived in our apartment building who was always trying to flirt with me. He would give us drugs and offer us jobs at the ice cream shop he managed. We also took molly together at a Phish concert, was I wearing stockings there? Suddenly my fears about not getting work done fell like onion skin. I rushed to my Instagram to check, scrolling memory after memory, hair color after hair color, purple to white to green to white again to golden blonde, until I came across the photo of me wearing a tie-dye shirt with a forest scene in the middle of it, and jean shorts, standing in front of some barrier, with the arena, crowd, and band in the background. My eyes are closed and I'm holding a tallboy.

"That awkward Phish concert moment when a Burlington Vermont man, who seemingly has a knife wound scar on his face, tells you you are from "Scary Barre [the town where Chinga and I grew up]"" the caption reads. I don't remember writing that. The photo is so dark it's hard to tell if I was wearing stockings under the jean shorts, but it's possible. I couldn't recall any other time we took molly together.

Shortly after that photo was taken by a very high Chinga, he grabbed my hand and squeezed it, promising me he'd take me to the front of the crowd so we could see the music better. He led me through the sea of people in psychedelic outfits with pink and yellow lights dripping down on them. We got close to the stage but those at the very front had, as Chinga later theorized, staked out their territory, and were protecting it fiercely. We couldn't get through that final barrier but had fun nevertheless.

"God, how are we friends? How did this happen?" Chinga exclaimed in the peak of our super-serotonin high We sat on the grass as the stage lights twirled around. I told him I preferred the music in the parking lot, a 1993 rap song blaring out of a damaged Honda Accord, to Phish, even on drugs. He laughed. Suddenly, the show was over and we were wired. We asked a taxi driver to take us to whatever club was open. He drove us to a restaurant in Aurora instead, or rather, the basement of a closed down restaurant, where the cabbie and his buddies were drinking beers. They sold us Coors Lights for 17 dollars apiece. I whispered to Chinga that I wanted to go home. I felt they were taking advantage of our intoxicated state. When the driver took us home, Chinga asked if he wanted to go to the strip club with him.

"I mean, I'll take you," the man said reluctantly.

"Chinga, why don't you just go home? We can finish up *Breaking Bad.* I don't think you should be out on your own right now."

I was thinking of when we were denied entry to a strip club just weeks earlier, because he was too intoxicated. I worried he wouldn't be allowed in, or that he would and would be taken advantage of financially or get into a fight. I thought about how his mother told me to watch out for him.

"You should listen to your wife," the cabbie scolded.

"She's not my wife," Chinga quickly snapped.

I huffed and rolled my eyes, continuing to look at the streaks of orange and red from cars moving alongside us through the darkness.

We pulled up in front of our apartment complex. Chinga announced he was going inside to get a six pack for him and the cabbie.

"I'll be right back," he told the driver.

While Chinga put the key in the door, I tried to get him not to go.

"Can't you see? He doesn't want to go. It's like five a.m. It's not safe out. Just stay home."

"I'll be fine," he sluffed, his eyes more glazed and distant, his smile more goofy than usual. "Don't worry."

"What if something happens? I promised your mom I'd look out for you."

He laughed. "Gina, I'll be fine. Go to bed."

I flicked on the light and watched Chinga open the fridge. I felt my heart pounding, the serotonin draining and my worry increasing.

"Please Chinga. I'm worried about you. You're fucked up. I mean, we both are. I don't want something bad to happen to you. I'm worried."

"Come here" He set the six pack on the counter, grabbed me and hugged me hard. "I love you." He rubbed my back. "Don't worry! Okay?"

Stunned, I replied, "I love you too," in a low tone, before mumbling, "Okay." Then the door closed behind him. I stood in the dark reminded of my father's modus operandi. Would my dad ever tell me he was proud of me, that he loved me? There was only one instance I could recall my dad actually uttering the phrase "I love you," and that was when I'd confronted him about feeling mistreated. I felt, always, that it was his way of shutting me up.

I swam through these memories treading lightly around Chinga's messages, attempting to force myself back to the task at hand, writing about murder. Get back to writing about the woman who killed her husband, to the jealous man who killed his lover, to the couple that plotted to kill a relative for money. But, ding! Chinga was in a whirlpool of thoughts and I didn't want to miss my chance at insight to his elusive mind, despite the fact that I knew he told me more than most, if not everyone else. He'd tell me secrets. Still, his mind had so many locked doors I was curious to peek through.

Krystal and Emine opened the door and a breeze from the window crept up my neck. Krystal's hair was wetter than before and slicked back. Emine's hair was also wet. They had a glow about them. They had clearly just had sex.

"Hey you two!"

I should start having sex romps and stop overthinking everything here on my trip, I thought. It's my breakup trip and I haven't fucked anyone. How pathetic am I? I'm talking to my crush of decades while in fucking Africa and I've been on my breakup trip for days now and I haven't banged anyone.

You should be fucking all kinds of guys, I reminded myself.

But the tinge of rejection burns hard, and I feared rejection of any kind. I thought back to vapor from the diffuser in Kyle and I's bedroom clouding the air as snowflakes fell outside, under that damn parking lot light. I had just tried to kiss Kyle and he told me his stomach hurt.

"It's because I'm deformed now, isn't it?"

"No, Bucky."

Vapor began rising within. "I saw you opened the KY bottle. Who are you sleeping with?"

"What are you talking about?"

"The fucking KY bottle you bought before my surgery. That we never used. It's been opened. The seal is off it."

"Oh, I didn't open it. Maybe it came that way."

"I Googled it. They come with sealed bottles."

"Well maybe someone at the factory fucked up. Come here," he said, hugging me close then kissing my forehead, "I love you."

After getting through security at the airport, we went into one of the convenience stores, where one would find gum, soda, and theoretically tampons. However, there were no tampons to be found. I asked the cashier. She shook her head no.

We went to the gate and waited. I don't remember why but we sat on the floor. I was feeling the kind of tired where things seemed too bright, beyond tired, too tired to sleep. Hungover from the booze, hungover from navigating a new area, drained from conversing with my childhood love. Under fluorescent lights, we heard passengers begin to fight in Arabic. I looked up as flight staff in suits and airplane pins passed by passengers sitting in the gate area. Some went up to them and yelled. The flight attendants seemed to dissociate as they walked into some kind of private door in the wall.

Krystal and I just looked at one another.

"I have to go pee," I said. "Let me know what I miss."

Krystal laughed.

I went to the bathroom, sat on the toilet, and started to pee.

Goddamn, I forgot to bring tissues again. Damn it. They were in my goddamn purse, sitting jerkily on the floor beside Krystal. I looked over to what appeared to be a toilet paper dispenser. It was silver in color and had a hole in the bottom, where I assumed toilet paper would live, but none was dangling out. I reached my hand. I didn't feel any paper. I pushed my hand in further and further until it felt like I had *something*. I twiddled my index and middle finger. There was definitely no toilet paper to be had, just something smooth and metal feeling.

"Fuck." I tried to retreat my hand, sliding it back through the hole, but it was crammed. Impulsively and with frustration, I forced it out. Some of my wrist's skin snagged on a jagged edge. It immediately began bleeding.

I looked at the hose on the floor and all the wet around it. I thought about trying to wipe myself, but between that and the blood, well, I figured that'd just make a worse mess. Instead, I just disgustingly pulled up my panties and ran out the stall to wash my bleeding finger under the sink. Holding my finger in the other hand, I walked out to Krystal. It was very stressful until I saw her. Then it was funny.

"Guess what I did."

I told her what happened and took the tissues from my bag, wrapping my hand in it.

"Ugh, gotta go back to cram wads of tissue up my vagina now."

What a mess.

When I returned, stuffed with paper and a hand wrapped in more, I saw a crowd gathering around our supposed gate.

"The flight should have taken off by now," Krystal said. There were visible bags under her eyes. I wasn't sure if it was just the lighting or a mix of that and actual exhaustion.

"Oh look." I pointed toward the gate. A woman in a blue pants suit with a skirt bottom came out the gate and walked hurriedly by the people gathering around. She appeared to avoid eye contact. Meanwhile, several ticket holders yelled at her in Italian and Arabic.

"What is going on?"

Two hours of Krystal and I sitting on the ground and zoning out later, some action stirred from the gate area. While no announcement was made, people did seem to be lining up. We stood up and walked over to the tail end of the line. I played with the flap of skin on my wrist. The area was dry but I worried about infection. No worries, I told myself, soon enough I'll be back home in my temporary Italian home cleaning it with alcohol.

"Here we go," I told Krystal as we passed through the gate, as if we were about to get on some stupid ride at Disney World or something. We walked through the tunnel until it abruptly ended at a hole to the outside, stars twinkling above us and beyond. A small propeller plane rested about 40 feet ahead. Not a fan of taking planes so small you have to walk to them, but at this point I didn't care. My orange Sicily bed was calling me. As was Amelia. I would have to get her after work. The dog sitter had already agreed to an extra day. In fact, they seemed ecstatic. They sent me videos of their 12-year-old in a red and white hat dancing around with Amelia to Mariah Carey's "All I Want for Christmas."

Christmas was indeed just days away.

We sat on the plane. The window in our aisle was smudged. I could see some lights but little else.

We waited for takeoff. We kept waiting. Suddenly, a man, seemingly the pilot, opened the door at the front of the aisle and said something in Arabic to a man in the front seat. He repeated the phrase and people began mumbling and yelling and standing up.

"What is going on?" I asked.

A man in the seat ahead of me stood and turned to me.

"Plane broken," he said.

Krystal and I turned to one another.

Then it was back to sitting on the floor while passengers yelled by the gates. At some point, at least an hour and a half later, one of the passengers was apparently told that the flight was canceled. We followed the crowd to an area where a member of Tunis Air, dressed up in stockings but with exhausted bags under her eyes, instructed us all to write our names on one single piece of paper that everyone on the flight had to pass around.

A Sicilian woman who reeked of Coco Chanel told us they were going to be putting us up in a hotel for the night. I gazed toward the airport walls and thought of the stars beyond, and a hotel maybe five minutes away. I imagined a Tunis version of the Marriott Inn, located in short proximity to the airport. Oh, how nice to have a warm bed and shower. At this point, I didn't care. We were all led outside and waited in silence amidst chattering in languages we didn't comprehend. What parts I did understand, I was tired of.

When the bus rolled up, the crowd groaned collectively. It looked like a bus I took on an eighth-grade field trip. You know the kind, with rugs on the floor and ceilings. This one was especially dingy. The windows, like in the airplane, were smudged. It looked like a rock band's bus at the end of a tour, maybe after some grimy orgy. Inside, it looked like an acid trip explosion, Rugged ceiling to floor and wall to wall, with those neon primary colored squiggles, circles, and triangles forever linked with the early 1990s.

Passengers were noticeably laughing at the aesthetic of the bus as they got on, along with more collective groans. A man, likely in his 30s, tall, dark and classically handsome, came in and looked me and Krystal up and down with lusty eyes as he passed. I got chills. When the bus filled, the driver got in and off we went, for what seemed like forever. Out the window was pure darkness. No lights from buildings or anywhere. Were we in the woods? A desert? Could be anywhere.

The man making lusty eyes kept staring back and Krystal and me. My brain envisioned the worst case scenario: him trying to break into our room to rape us, or from his porn-obsessed perspective, to have sex with us, which we would be super psyched to do. I know I was making a lot of jumps in logic, but experience is a hell of a teacher. My intuition screamed at me to make sure he didn't see our room number, to turn invisible now.

"Did you see that look?" I whispered to Krystal. She nodded.

Eventually the bus started slowing down and turned. The passengers audibly deflated once again. The people sitting in front row must have recognized the hotel, perhaps they were locals, we later gathered. We pulled up to the front entrance of a pretty run-down looking hotel, seemingly in the middle of nowhere.

"Let's try to run in before some of these dudes to get our room," I whispered. As we got off the bus, the man I was nervous over stood hovering around the bottom of the bus where the suitcases were stored, waiting in line for his gear. We just had carry-ons, so luckily could just walk right in. We were the second group in line. The lobby felt empty and cold.

As the front desk woman handed me the key to our room just around the corner, I whispered, "Do you have tampons?"

The woman cocked her head, "No, sorry."

"Pads?"

"No." Her lips formed a frown.

"Do you know when the flight is going to be?"

"They said sometime tomorrow. They will let you know by 2 pm tomorrow."

I sighed. "Okay, thanks."

Our hotel room had a sixties vibe with a musky smell, and another wet floor and bathroom hose. I was just glad to have a warm bed. Or at least *a* bed. It was so cold that night and our blanket was so flimsy, we ended up cuddling for warmth. It wasn't particularly comfortable, given the toilet paper crammed up my insides and the drafty air, but it was better than sleeping on the airport floor.

Thoughts about my rapist kept me awake. I felt like he was close to me. What if he was visiting nearby? *No, Gina, that's a crazy thought* (spoiler: I learned years later, he was indeed in Tunis when Krystal and I were). My mind went to a story my mom told me as a kid. She said a "bad man" "did something" to her cousin and took pictures of her while she was "asleep." So, seeing as her mom, my aunt, worked at a dress shop run by the Gambino family, they asked for a favor.

"They scared him," my mom said. "It was a different time, the 70s. You don't want to ask favors from people like that but sometimes it's good to know people like that, in rare cases like this."

God, I wish she were alive when that happened to me. She would have fought for justice. It was always in her blood. She would have cared, her love for me was fiercely in her blood too. If her love was a color it would be red, intense and strong. My dad's, in contrast, was pale blue, not menacing, but distant and cold. I became an annoying pimple, a growth he was responsible for, linked to, until his death. It was never clear if he enjoyed the connection or cared if it would end.

Krystal's leg knelt close to the back of mine and I found myself at ease. My thoughts disjointed. I saw red and blue kaleidoscopes until I faded out.

✂

Light seeped in from the window. I remained blanket-wrapped with phone in hand, trying to connect to the internet. There didn't appear to be any wifi.

"Uh oh," Krystal giggled from beyond the bathroom door. She opened it up and shouted, "I got my period too!"

"Oh no!" We locked eyes and laughed. "We synched up."

"Looks like we'll both be cramming toilet paper in our vaginas."

"Dear god, maybe we can ask someone about it on the bus today. Somebody's gotta have tampons or pads or *something*," I said. "I need to find out about the wifi anyway. Maybe I'll investigate that too."

I did, they didn't, and there was no wifi. I logged onto my international plan and messaged the dogsitter and my job about our delay. One more day of dogsitting, sorry and please. I told my job there was no wifi so I couldn't work if I wanted to. I was trapped at a hotel until later that day, sorry and thanks.

With that behind me, I wouldn't repeat the previous day's struggles. I immediately felt more relaxed, like I'd just thrown my laptop in the ocean or something.

Pretty soon, Krystal and I were sitting by the pool sipping beers with Arabic labels. Men hovered the perimeter, but no sign of the creepy guy from the bus. Where was he? I peered up at the rows of windows in the hotel. The curtains could be covering up anything.

I chugged my beer thinking about my job. I was nervous. Days of being semi-present at work with no warning. What if they thought I was lying, half-assing things, maybe using drugs? What if I lost my job?

Without a word between us, Krystal caught on, "Are you obsessing about your job again?"

I laughed, "Yes."

"Don't worry, you work so hard, you deserve some time off."

She took a box of fresh dates from her travel bag. "May as well eat these."

I put one in my mouth and never have I ever had a date so good.

My phone dinged, an email from my editor, who'd just started his workday. "Looks like you're having quite the adventure, no worries." I read it aloud to Krystal.

"See? You need to relax more. They like you. I'll go grab you another beer."

The hotel aesthetic mirrored the Copacabana way after it was cool. Like past its heyday and knee-deep in its seedy, bug and bullet-filled days. "I bet this place was pretty rad in the sixties."

Blood was filling up the tissues crammed in our crotches. We decided to try to scrounge the area for tampons or something better than… that. We asked a few of the people on our bus. They didn't have tampons either. Or pads. Or anything. We resigned to wadding up more toilet paper, the scratchy kind to boot.

The crowd from our plane crowded around the front desk demanding answers until the acid-soaked bus rolled up around 6 pm and we piled in. I didn't see the man with the lusty eyes. Perhaps he was a hallucination. A fear based on my 2010 attack. Surely, it wouldn't be the first time.

The dinky plane worked enough to get us across the sea to Sicily, but one of the lights above our heads kept flickering the whole way like a strobe light, and the plane was shaking so much I feared we would plummet into the dark water beneath us, the fish and plankton unmoved by our demise.

That night, it felt so nice to be in my temporary orange bed, next to a close friend. Our adventure had pulled that bond even closer, yet I couldn't help feeling distant. I felt closer to David, or any dude I'd fucked, despite the *lack* of emotional bonding, comparatively. Does my body just rely on the hormones that sex gives me, like a fucking animal. Or am I simply incapable of feeling super close to people I am not fucking?

I've always wanted intimacy, but now it seemed further away than ever before. As a child, I instinctively knew something was missing from my life. It was definitely love. I had love, but it wasn't the warm love of a sunny palm tree, it was cold like falling snow. I could sense the palm tree love radiating from friends' parents, even in snow-covered trailers. While my parents looked down at some of my friends' families, I would have traded my own father for a man with a Bud Light in his hand and a mustache filled with chewing tobacco if he would have just been proud of me for existing. My mom was school and career motivated. That was what was important for her, so that was what was important for me. "Don't worry about these relationships. They won't matter to you someday, you'll be successful," she'd tell me.

But those relationships ended up mattering to me very much. I still think about them all the time. It's connection I want. Call me a sucker but I'll take the roots over the flowers. That's success. But how to un-ingrain the ingrained to get there?

# Ted

"Did you have an arancini yet?" multiple dark haired men in speedos messaged me on Tinder. It was Dec. 13, Arancini Day.

I saw their messages upon awakening, Amelia nestled between Krystal and me under the orange cover. Her body heat made me reluctant to get up into the cold room. I set my phone back on the table and closed my eyes. It was seven a.m. No need to get up. Please rest. My brain was telling me it was time to get up and work. Time to get up and be productive or feel guilty about not being productive. Those were the only choices in life, according to the little capitalist worm in my head.

*No*, I fought back. *Sleep, Gina, sleep.*

*No*, the worm argued. *You should write. Your writing career will never heal if you don't start working on some new projects. Furthermore, bitch, your heart will never heal if you don't start working on some new dating prospects.*

Krystal and I walked down to the main road that morning. I'd forgotten the arancini texts, but the landscape made sure to remind me. There were carts filled with arancini - a classic Sicilian dish, deep fried rice balls, typically with ragu at the center and sometimes also with meat -everywhere. The streets were loaded with people holding balls wrapped in white tissue paper or cellophane, digging in, chomping away with sauce spilling out on their pants like blood.

Afterward we went to Ballaro, probably Palermo's most famous open-air market. Krystal picked up some fresh veggies and fish: one of them large and pink.

"I'm going to cook up a stew while you work today," she told me.

I sat at my computer, writing a story about the alleged disturbing porn habits of Brendan Dassey's brother.

*In Season 2 of <u>Making a Murderer</u>, Steven Avery's post-conviction lawyer, Kathleen Zellner, pointed the finger at Brendan Dassey's brother as a possible suspect in the murder of photographer Teresa Halbach, in part because of his alleged interest in violent porn.*

*The first season of the Netflix docu-series was released in 2015, and it raised many questions about the convictions of Avery and his nephew Brendan Dassey, who were both sentenced to life in prison in 2007 for the death of Halbach in 2005.*

*The second part of the docu-series shows how challenging it can be to overturn a conviction, and focuses heavily on Zellner's investigation into what really happened to Halbach. Zellner explains that her investigation into the truth left her with some questions about Brendan Dassey's brother Bobby. She talked frequently about Bobby's alleged interest in violent pornography.*

*Zellner said there is evidence that shows Bobby downloaded violent porn.*

*"We have found thousands and thousands of images that could only have been accessed by Bobby Dassey," Zellner said. She showed a document from her investigation team that showed he made internet searches like "11 year old sex," "rotten girl," "gun to head," and "f--- preteen girl."*

*"Torture, bondage, pedophilia, nightmare stuff," she said. "Fascination with death. ... decapitated girls, things like that. I mean, this is astounding."*

*Zellner accused Bobby of compulsively making such searches for hundreds of hours.*

I pondered how often investigators look over such evidence, how easy it is to overlook hard drives or other items of note, particularly if they are from a small rural town and are boomers who don't fully know how to read internet history or cookies. Or if they already have a suspect in mind. Or if they don't care.

It's so easy to overlook evidence or connections. Television detectives put clues together like Lego sets when really it's the opposite: rural and inexperienced or overwhelmed and jaded city cops. I thought of the investigators who were supposed to be working on finding the "Park Slope Rapist" in Brooklyn. Posters of his sketch were plastered up around the neighborhoods of Bay Ridge, Park Slope, and Sunset Park just months after my rapist abducted me in Park Slope and took me back to Sunset Park where he lived. When I went to the police, they were able to connect him to two other incidents. I learned he attacked another girl in Bay Ridge and another in Park Slope. He was originally indicted for all three incidents. One detective told me he likely raped many others. Awaiting what I assumed would be the trial against him, I saw these posters and heard horror stories of a man who looked like my attacker going after strangers in dresses and skirts, petite white girls, in the same three areas. His height, his build, it was all the same. I'd call the Crime Stoppers line from the studio of my job, shutting the door behind me, hoping my coworker wouldn't turn on any studio mics.

"Yeah, but that man is Algerian and the Park Slope Rapist is Latino."

"I described him as Latino though," I said, "or Italian." So did the other women. "Nobody is going to describe a stranger as Algerian. Mediterranean maybe."

They didn't even take down a report number. They didn't log it. I know they didn't log it. I doubt they cared. I doubt they looked into it. They were probably bogged down with crimes and probably didn't care. I was addicted to drugs at the time and one of the other survivors was a sex worker. Why would cops, in 2010, even pretend to care?

Krystal came into the room holding a red plastic plate in her hand. Atop it were pinkish-orange chunks of flesh.

"A little snack for you." She set the dish on the desk, right beside my laptop.

"What's this?"

"It's some fish."

I touched one of the jellonious pieces of meat. It was cold.

"Is it raw?"

"Yeah, it's el crudo! It's good."

"Ahh thank you."

I picked one up and placed it on my tongue. It was soft and fresh, like sushi but slightly different.

She left the room and I heard her happily humming as water boiled on the stove. I ate more chunks of fish flesh, growing fonder of the taste with each bite.

I continued to write about violent porn. I mined an interview I was present for while covering a true crime festival with criminal profiler and former FBI special agent John Douglas, who was the inspiration for Holden in *Mind Hunter*. I wrote:

*Experts say violent pornography doesn't cause crime, but can encourage someone with a predilection towards violence.*

*"What pornography will do is fuel the fantasy,"* I quoted John. *"It's not the cause of it, it just fuels an already screwed-up mind. You could say the same thing about a violent movie. Did the movie cause it or did it fuel this guy's thinking?"*

Krystal walked into the room and picked up her sweatshirt, which was folded neatly atop the bed.

"Hey, that fish was really good. What kind of fish was it?"

Her face slightly blushed from wine, she smiled and shrugged.

"You don't know?"

My mind dove into a pool of memories of my mom telling me to be careful eating raw fish. This was before eating sushi was mainstream, at least suburban mainstream. My mind also rushed to the *Simpsons* episode where Homer almost died from eating a slice of bad fish. "But people have to take classes to learn what parts can be eaten raw or not," I blurted, "Not all fish can be eaten raw." My heart rate began to accelerate, I felt a rush of adrenaline.

"What if we die from this?"

"I'm sure it's fine," she said.

"It was a pink fish right?" I began googling images of common fish in the area, pink ones. The first name that came up was the scrofa, or scorpion fish, described as a venomous fish, quite poisonous. I pulled up the photo. Scorpaena scrofa. "Looked like this right?"

"Yeah," she said.

"Oh no. We should go to the doctors or something or the hospital."

"Maybe just the drug store. I saw one nearby with a neon plus sign on our walk."

"Okay." My palms started to sweat.

I shot my boss a message over slack, in my head thinking it could be one of my last: "Accidently ate raw poisonous fish. Going to go to the pharmacist to make sure we are okay."

"Oh no!" she said. "Good luck."

I was grouchy as we walked to the pharmacy. I was short with Krystal.

I am going to die. I am poisoned, I told myself.

"Mangio pesce crudo," I barked in panic at the pharmacist.

"Mangiamo… Oh what was the name?" Krystal asked.

I pulled my phone from my back pocket and opened the browser. It was still on the photo of the fish. The scorpion fish. The red thorny fish sitting on the bottom of a sea, pebbles surrounding his angry face.

"Voglio scorpaena crudo," I told the pharmacist.

She looked horrified. "When you are in your country and you want that, where do you go?"

"The grocery store?'

She looked even more disturbed.

I held the photo up for her, "Mangiamo, crudo."

"Oh," she said. "Okay, okay, okay. That's okay. They cut. It's okay."

Now, I could have just taken the rest of the day off. My boss would have obviously been okay with it. But did I? No. I worked the last hour and a half, shaken up and filled with adrenaline, like a chump. I wrote yet another daily story about a man who'd murdered his girlfriend. I reached out to the area police department, got a quick confirmation of the basic facts: girlfriend shot in the head, boyfriend charged with second degree murder, motive = jealousy. No lawyer, held without bond, dating for just two months, girlfriend's sister described her to me over Facebook as "kind, the type of girl who would give her shirt off her back to a stranger."

Krystal continued to cook, humming to music in her headphones, chopping onions and whatnot and throwing them in boiling water. Plop, plop, plop. There she was, living like a European while I worked like an American. No, I corrected myself, she's living like an American too. I'm just too frozen in my own head to live outside of it sometimes. As for cooking, that takes a certain level of warmness for me to even attempt in front of another. I'm more comfortable fucking someone than having them watch me cook. If sex is first base, cooking is like third.

Kyle was actually very kind and patient with my cooking, despite his culinary school background, which could have made him more snooty than previous exes. In fact, he told me I was the best at making eggs. He said eggs are one of the easiest things to fuck up, thus proving I'm not a bad cook. I'd make him egg sandwiches every morning I had time.

I'd nudge the egg onto its side as it sizzled in the black pan, sun from the window heating up my right thigh in our cramped kitchen, the egg lightly browned but I knew it was still soft and gooey on the inside. Two pieces of bread popped out the toaster and I threw them on the ceramic plate, spatulated the egg and plopped it on a slice. I placed the other slice on top and pushed down gently. Then I'd cut the sandwich in half, and yellow blood dripped down the sides. I brought it to Kyle sitting at his computer chair.

"Thanks Bucky."

Cut scene to us making perogies together from scratch, spreading out newspaper across the dining room table so we wouldn't make a mess, a bowl of water turned cloudy, hand rolling the perogies and placing them on trays, pressing lines on them with the pointy edge of a fork.

"I love doing this kind of stuff," I gushed. "It makes me feel so normal."

Moments like this made me feel whole. Like a functional person, a real girlfriend. It wasn't always like this.

"What the hell is wrong with you," an ex asked when I was 20, "do you even know how to cook pasta?"

I fell into myself and blushed, "No."

He was so repulsed by my lack of kitchen knowledge he stopped letting me help. Sometimes he'd let me cut up zucchini, but he'd say I did that wrong too. Mostly I washed dishes.

"Didn't your mom ever teach you to fucking cook?"

He was not as patient as Kyle, but more patient than my mother. I always *wanted* to cook. I remember learning how to make crepes in 7th grade home economics class. My mom only let me make them at home once, under a lot of supervision and pressure to not make a mess.

Then she was too tired for me to try again until, well ever. I was home some during college on breaks but she wouldn't let me cook. Then during my third year of college she got sick again, so of course it was not appropriate to make a mess of the kitchen. Better to let Dad boil frozen peas and buy pre-cooked chicken from Hannaford's.

"You have to make a mess to learn," Kyle would always say. "You can't become good at it without a few messes. And even when you are good, there's still messes to be made."

After Krystal left, I was left to my Tinder and exPats group for socialization. And WhatsApp with all my boys who shifted from Tinder, including Ted.

"I'll take you to the best pizza around," he messaged.

He brought me to a small pizza place on my block. Was it the best though?

"It's the cheapest place," he said as we took a seat.

I told him about the fish fiasco and how horrified the pharmacist looked.

"What did you tell her?"

I began describing all the ways we tried to tell her we ate raw fish.

"Oh god," he said. "It kind of sounds like you were saying you want raw sex. Like afternoon sex."

"Oh geez," I laughed.

We ordered two entire pizzas, each costing about four dollars, and drank a couple of beers. Then he drove me through a tunnel of trees to Mondello, where we walked the beach. It was about sixty degrees, cold for the area, so it was empty, but the city beside us made for a light show of reflections.

It was all nice. Pretty. Gorgeous. All the descriptions. Still, my suspicious, always critical mind couldn't help think he did this for all the women. But who cares right? Don't I play by the same playbook with most of the guys I see? Repeat the same jokes sometimes? What's the difference?

On the drive back to Palermo, he asked, "Are you romantic?" I looked out the window and saw tree after tree, each one looking no different than the last and laughed. "No." I wasn't quite sure what that even meant, really. I didn't care to ask.

We parked close to my apartment and walked toward the music of Vucciria. African men leaned against mopeds as large speakers blasted music. The crowd was gathered so closely in the alley it was like going through a birthing canal of bodies to get a drink. We got cheap fig wine and found a spot by one of the speakers with space to move around.

Ted kept trying to get me to say a phrase in Italian. I would try and try but couldn't roll my 'r's, which he found hilarious. We were dancing by one of the speakers when we kissed. "Despacito" was playing and I warped to another world. A nice kick in the butt. I instantly felt less alone, tongue crammed in my mouth and all. The purple wine in my belly warmed me up, and continued to as he walked me home through the back alleys, past graffiti of a sword and roses.

When we got to my pad what had seemed fun during a makeout blossomed into a rose of indifference. The sexual chemistry didn't quite match up. He was attractive but I just wasn't feeling it. I did not take off my bra. I mumbled something about cancer when he tugged at it and he put up no fight.

In the morning we began talking and I don't know how it came about, but I said I was always cold and wished I had a heater, not just the space heater.

"What are you, an idiot? There's a heater right there." he pointed at the thing on the wall.

I laughed, "I thought it was an air conditioning unit."

I was offended by his comment but refrained from getting upset. Maybe it was a language barrier thing. Or maybe he was just a dick. Or maybe he genuinely found me to be an idiot. Or all of the above. Hard to tell.

And then from idiocracy to roses and guitars.

"You know, I think you are romantic," he told me. I felt my shoulders tense as I backed myself away and turned over on the bed.

"Why do you say that?" I danced my fingers around the orange blanket.

"Our first kiss was to "Despacitio" and that's pretty romantic."

I cringed, raised my shoulders up in disgust. I had to try not to laugh.

"Well, I didn't kiss because of the song," I said. "Jesus."

If anything, I wanted to say, I wished it was another song. I kissed him because I was drunk. Because I wanted to connect with someone. Regardless of the "romantic" comments, how nice it was to curl up into his arms and feel the coziness of cuddling. It had surely been a bit and he was a good enough cuddler.

"Can you do me a favor?" he said as he rubbed my bare shoulder softly. "Go get me a cappuccino and a cornetti? I'll get you next time."

I shrugged and said sure.

## Otto

Unsatisfied with that sexual experience, I decided I needed to fuck someone I like.

Perhaps a German would be a little less into romance than an Italian? Maybe I, an American, who is conditioned to be disgusted by most romantic gestures, would feel comfortable in the arms of a rigid German man.

I was chatting with Chinga on Facebook while sipping a Dixie cup of wine, waiting for the right time to walk down to Vuccuria to meet Otto. I told Chinga how strange Tinder was in Sicily. When we lived together we'd both be on Tinder and would compete to see who would get the most matches. It was me, which, duh, that's just normal for women or female presenting people. We'd screenshot our most absurd matches: for me, it was a man named Brent who was on a bed in his selfie, wearing a shirt with the giant phrase "family" across it, his lips very moist, and an outlet beside his bed with four outlets and one item requiring electricity blocking the other three outlets.

"Wanna to sit on my face?" was the first thing Brent sent me. Chinga and I spent a lot of time trolling him.

I messaged Chinga that I was about to carry a bottle of wine down to a street party.

"You can drink on the street there? Damn, America sucks."

Before leaving, I checked my email. One was from a literary agent, one of many I'd queried recently and one of three who'd offered to look at my latest manuscript.

Heartbeat increasing, I opened it.

*Hi Gina,*

*Thanks so much for the chance to read your manuscript. After careful consideration, I have decided that this is not a good match for me.*

*Best,*
*Charles.*

I sighed.

"Of course," I mumbled. "If only I didn't fuck up with the agent I did have."

I walked down to Vuccira with an open bottle of wine, plastic cups stacked inside my purse. As I got to the crowd, I saw Otto standing out with his peppered hair, his neck draped in a dark purple scarf.

We shook hands, I offered him a glass of wine and he said he rarely drinks but encouraged me to go ahead.

"How long are you here again?" he asked, sipping on a red plastic cup filled with what I assumed was water.

"Two months."

"In Palermo both months?"

"No, December here. Next month I go to Bagheria."

"You want to go to Bagheria?! Really?! Why the hell would you book a month there?"

"I don't know. It looks nice."

"It's not. It's run down."

"Is it dangerous?" I asked, uncorking my bottle and pouring myself a drink.

"No, but nothing to do."

"But I'm a writer, nothing to do is okay sometimes. "Now's party time. Then will be writing time I guess."

Even though literally no editor nor agent cared if I ever wrote another word again, minus my day job editors. At this point, nobody was expecting any books. I could give up and no one would miss me. They'd barely notice.

"I mean there is *nothing* to do there," Otto insisted, clanging my wine bottle with the nail of his index finger for extra emphasis. "Feel like checking out a few parties?"

"I'm definitely up for that."

He took me to a very DIY looking event that had a suggested donation of a euro to get in. There were a few art sculptures, one made of old televisions, and a courtyard filled with wheat paste murals, one of a girl in a wedding dress holding a gun and a man who looked like a demon dog. People danced in a room partially outside lined with warm Christmas lights. The DJ was smiling. We sat on a bench and chatted until Otto led me down crowded Palermo alleyways to a modest looking bar behind a closed cafe in a parking lot filled with tiny pickup trucks.

"It's sort of like an art collective place. You're supposed to be a member to get in, or you can just pay. Or, you can get a membership that lets you into any of these events for free. It's not too expensive"

"How much is a membership?" I asked.

"Nine euro."

"Oh yeah, I'll do that."

I forked over the money and got a laminated card that said a bunch of things I couldn't understand. I smiled and put it into my back jeans pocket. "Grazie."

We walked inside. The bar was blaring techno but very few people were there, a couple bodies scattered about the dance floor while strobe lights rolled around maniacally off beat. My eyes were drawn to a black triangle on the dancefloor.

"It's a window," Otto said as we walked toward it.

"What?" I asked. I looked down through the glass and saw a stream below. There was a piece of seaweed swimming in the current like a defiant eel.

"Water runs under this entire city like that," Otto explained.

I drunkenly thought of Chinga and suddenly had the urge to call him. Instead, I drank. Soon the wine bottle was empty and I didn't want to seem like too much of a lush, plus I could feel

Otto's energy levels decreasing. He walked me home. I said he could come up if he wanted. It didn't feel like he was interested in me, though I did find him attractive. Wasn't looking to hook up but wasn't against it.

"Sure, I'll take a look at your place. Always curious to see the Airbnb's targeted to tourists."

I opened the door and he started laughing.

"What the hell?" he asked as Amelia ran up and jumped upon him. "Hallo! Hallo!"

"What?" I smirked.

"The blackboard." he pointed at the "note to self: don't fuck anyone in the mafia."

I laughed as my phone buzzed in my pocket. Now that we were back on the wifi, the messages were coming in. "Oh yeah, just a joke."

He gave me a hug, said we should hang soon, and left me in the apartment. I looked at my phone. The messages were mostly from Chinga. I washed off my makeup, put on astringent and all my night creams, put my hair up in a top bun and sat on the bed, hugging what was left of the limoncello bottle.

I opened my laptop and asked Google "What time is it in Denver?"

It was six p.m. in the mile high city.

I messaged Chinga, "You are one of my best homies and I am glad you are still in my life. I miss hanging as pals in the real world."

Then I shut the laptop, embarrassed by the sincerity and vulnerability of the wine-soaked message. It was kind of out of character, but I knew he knew the sentiment was always there. Would it be too much in written form though? I turned out the lights and immediately heard the ding of an incoming message.

"Haha we will have to hang sometime somewhere in the future! I agree!" he wrote back. His message popped up on my lock screen. I didn't open it. I smiled, turned around, hugged Amelia, and fell asleep easily.

♪♪

    I began going to language exchange nights at Cavu, the same bar Krystal and I brought Amelia the night she arrived. Not only did they allow pet dogs, but strays would wander in too. Those dogs were just like bar patrons, aloof, polite, and just like some of them, mooched drinks off others. And I respect that. One was a quiet white Chow Chow mix who wandered into the bar and sat down toward the back before curling up and taking a nap while a DJ spun loud techno just feet away.

    I quickly learned that while some used the meetup to learn language, most of the members (i.e. men) attended in hopes of picking up foreigners. In fact, the majority of attendees were men. I met two Norwegian women about a decade younger than me, a sweet Lithuanian couple, and a few stiff tall German men. Other men, Italians and alike, gravitated toward the blondes. I was happy to have my hair dark and to look Italian. Sure, I loved attention, but I preferred to not be a novelty.

    Ted moved from sitting next to me after telling someone in Italian that he fucked me (I didn't understand much of the language, but I instinctively knew the dynamic), then started hitting on some of the blonde Eastern Europeans.

    I wasn't offended but it was extremely juvenile for someone who was like 35.

    "What area do you live in?" one of Ted's friends asked.

    "Close, via Vittorio Emanuel," I said sipping my drink, a local red wine. "But next month I'm going to be staying in Bagheria."

    The man's eyes widened. He put his hand up and gestured it downward, dramatically.

    "Porque?"

    "Everyone keeps saying that! Is it a bad area?"

    "It's not bad. Just run down. And boring."

    Ted chimed in.

"I'll get you a cheap place in Palermo, Gina! Please, Please!"

His friends chimed in.

"Yes, stay in Palermo! Is better!"

"Stay! Stay!"

"Ted runs a service for tourists. He'll get you place. Cheap, cheap!"

"Please."

"Okay, okay, Grazie."

That night, Ted and I had sex again and the musical aspects of our short-lived fucking history grew even worse:

At his apartment building, not far from the train station, he sat in a chair holding his guitar playing "Hotel California," staring at me with gentle eyes the whole time he played and sang. I'm certain there are women out there who would love this, who are maybe reading this rolling their eyes at me but I CAN'T. I don't know what to do. Where do I look? What should I do? Do I fucking clap? I just smiled and nodded as he played, wishing for it all to stop but when it did he played another, then another.

Then he kissed me.

"Let's go to the bedroom," I said. I was more interested in him putting down the guitar than fucking him. I just wanted desperately to get away from *all that.* But *all that* amplified when we entered his bedroom. He put on a romantic sounding musical playlist. I looked at his bed and its silk comforter. I sighed.

As "You're beautiful, it's true" was playing, he kept pawing at me, trying to get me to take off my bra.

"No, I had cancer," I said. I wasn't sure if he fully registered that. I told him no. It wasn't the same as with David. I guess it was because, in part, I didn't really like Ted. For me, taking off my bra and showing my most painful flaws was more intimate than fucking.

I dissociated while we had sex, trying to imagine other music, any other music: Easy E, Nine Inch Nails, Too Short, Amy Grant, Notorious B.I.G., fucking Tag Team, Vengaboys, Selena

Gomez, The Fat Boys, Toby Keith, Artic Monkeys, fucking anything else. It would have been easy, in theory, to ask him to change the music, but for whatever reason I just didn't. I wasn't sure I could fully articulate it. As Ted snored next to me, I pondered if hookup culture in Sicily was romance culture. Like if the stuff we do when we are in love, and only sometimes in America, is what they do when they are just fucking someone there. Or maybe Italians just think Americans are idiots and this is what we want to hear to get into bed.

I woke up with Amelia at our feet. He made me pasta for breakfast, shirtless and wearing athletic track pants. I ate while looking out his kitchen window at the spiky tall mountains. I told him I had to walk Amelia and had work to do.
"I'm going to get you a place around here, which will be good for both of us. Real cheap. And near me too." He winked.

"Bellissimo. Grazie." I said.

Ted's neighborhood was very pale and filled with garbage. It had a grit and grime feel to it, but not a dangerous vibe. I guess the best way to describe it is "run down."

I walked over a few piles of trash and literal feces in the hot sun as Amelia peed, creating a trail of urine that entered a crack in the sidewalk. I felt filthy following the fuck session. I felt filthier from the romantic music than I did after times in my life when I let a man choke me and spit on me. That was hot, fun, and natural. This was not natural. This was a crime. I wanted to let loose and fuck Italians, but I didn't like so far how they talked and acted, even though I'd only fucked one.

Speaking of crimes, I had plans with Otto that very night and I felt guilty for overlapping possible sex days. But who would know the difference really? And who cares?

☠

When I brought Otto home that night, he almost barked at me, "Why is your patio door open? That's dangerous. Someone could come in. It's not that safe here."

"It seems pretty safe," I mumbled, shutting the door. "Plus, it's the second floor. How would they come up?"

"Ladders."

Soon we were watching an Irish show he grew up liking on my laptop. Not much later we were kissing and rolling around and I instantly felt more comfortable than with Ted; Otto was emotionally detached from his physical actions.

"What's this on your arm? A gun?"

"It's a writer motto," I mumbled, kissing his neck.

As our lips resumed touching, I mumbled that I had cancer and would understand if he wasn't interested in hooking up.

"Oh that's silly," he said, and led my hand to a lump on his head. "It's benign. We all have our things."

Still, I kept my bra on when we had sex.

As the sun peered into the curtains of our eyelids the next morning, Otto reminded me not to go to Bagheria.

"Okay, okay. I'm not. Yes, everyone keeps telling me that." I hesitated before saying, "There's a guy here who is a landlord, kinda, and he said he could get me a sweet deal on a place to stay."

Otto laughed before saying, "Oh, you must mean Ted."

My eyes shifted back to Otto's hands and his fingers wrapped around my own above the comforter. "Yeah."

"I'm sure you slept with him too, huh?"

I sighed.

"He loves trying to sleep with *all* the foreign girls."

"I did," I admitted. "And it was very cheesy. Him playing guitar and saying romantic things. It was much too much."

"That's Italians for ya."

He left and I showered.

Buzzz.

I rang Ted's doorbell. He buzzed me in, toweling off his hair and blowing a kiss to a blonde woman leaving his place. I felt a tinge of hurt, like a papercut, but a really small one.

*Whatever, Gina, who cares. You don't like him and you just hooked up with Otto.*

We hugged hello.

"Ciao, Ciao."

He put a gray fitted sweater over his white t and yawned as we walked down his stairway.

We walked about a block and a half, past the train station and under a walkway through a little tunnel featuring a religious looking statue in the corner, not far from what appeared to be dumped out cat litter stuffed with clumps of shit. He led me to an apartment building located in one of the four inner walls of a parking lot, the middle of a plaza. It was above a grocery store, adjacent to an Asian market, a pillow store, two one-euro stores, a café, and a bunch of wholesale clothing shops selling tight shirts decorated with rhinestone phrases like "Angel" and "Baby" hugging white mannequins under bright fluorescent lights.

A man named Gaetano wearing a ribbed sweater and jeans welcomed us at the door. He and Ted talked in Italian in the elevator. I could see through their gesturing that Gaetano was trying to gather if Ted was sleeping with me, as if this was a typical experience. I felt pimped out but Ted promised this place would be half the price of an Airbnb, so who cared at this point? I couldn't unfuck him. And now I could inform any friend who inquired what it was like to fuck an Italian that their hookup culture is fake romance culture. Well, based on a one man study.

He brought me to an apartment located on the second floor. The only window was two feet wide, one foot tall and looked out to the hallway. It had wooden inner shutters and a metal grate for a screen. The apartment was essentially a studio, a small living room area with an Ikea looking couch, a plastic table with two plastic chairs adjacent from a small kitchenette area with a mini fridge tucked into the cabinets. Two cloudy plastic dividers built into the wall partially separated the bedroom from the rest of the space.

The bathroom shower was bigger than mine and the hot water tank looked larger.

"Yeah, you should have more hot water than in your place now," Ted said.

I smiled. "Sold."

☕

Most of my December mornings started out the same way.

I'd walk and get a foamy cappuccino with Amelia. I'd be impatient the whole time waiting in line, frustrated trying to communicate. Hurry up. Give me my check. Ugh, how do I say that again? Am I pronouncing it wrong? I felt like a chunk of glass was between me and everyone.

Then I'd walk down to Giardino Garibaldi, a park within feet of my place where the oldest and the biggest Ficus tree in Europe lives. Its branches spread out like spider webs, elephant trunks. I'd think about how much I missed the people I loved, wondered if I'd ever get the connection I crave, if I'd ever be able to express and receive it in a healthy way.

Then I'd walk down to the water and take pictures. I loved how the blue and green would kiss, like two different shades of paint mixing to create a new one. I'd upload the pictures to my Insta stories, but they never fully captured what I saw with the hole in my eyes. Sometimes I'd wander all the way up to Teatro Massimo Palermo. At this time, the steps were covered in what looked from afar to be a red carpet. However, up close it was clear that it was a pile of strategically placed poinsettias clustered on the stairs. They transformed into the mirage of a fluffy, elevated, red carpet.

I'd write stories for work, primarily of men killing their girlfriends. Or at least the police deemed them boyfriend and girlfriend. It's convenient; anyone who is dating or has some sort of sexual relationship but not married is deemed boyfriend and girlfriend. It's just easier to report. But are all these so-called couples *actually* couples? Like if David or Otto or Ted killed me, media reports would call them my boyfriend because, I'd assume, the police would. Though, that obviously doesn't mean they were. They really jump the gun on the ole "what are we" conversation.

✝

    Friends reached out to me on the morning of Christmas Eve to see if I could see the volcano from where I was. Mount Etna was apparently erupting, spewing lava. But it was very far away. It had been quiet since its previous eruption in July and now decided to have a fit on Christmas, like so many of us do. Like I have.

    Otto told me that I could hang out with one of his roommates, who was also alone for Christmas. That was a nice thought, I thought, but the idea of putting in energy to make a new friend seemed draining to me. Especially if they were connected to someone I liked. What if we went out drinking together and I flirted with guys? What if we didn't get along and she told Otto I sucked? I was too anxious about it.

    I told him thank you, but I just wanted to write.

    Almost immediately my stupid brain began playing cheesy movies of what kind of wonderful Christmas Eve I could be having with this stranger. If I had said yes, me and this woman would have shared few drinks together and laughed and joked and talked and bonded and gone to Vucciria and drank more and people-watched and just have had the best time.

    Then my brain cut to a more realistic horror movie of what could happen: I meet up with the woman and there is a language barrier and we don't communicate properly. It's awkward and I get grouchy over the situation. She reads that as me being a bitch and tells Otto she doesn't like me and the whole affair is over. Or maybe me gushing about him would lead her to fall for him. It has happened before.

    Maybe it's better I don't even bother, I told myself. It's safer to be alone.

    Amelia and I wandered around a green park full of palm trees, next to the sea full of merging turquoise and teal patches. Waves bashed the rocks alongside the trail.

Back at the AirBnb, I sat at the desk and took a deep sigh. Now that I was back on Wifi, text messages and the like were rolling in. I looked at my WhatsApp. It was a message from Otto.

"Good luck writing today. Also, don't work all day. Life is not just about productivity, ya know."

He sent it along with a photo of him holding homemade Christmas cookies. I smiled. Why *was* I working on Christmas? Because, I reminded myself, writing doesn't let you down. Writing doesn't betray you. Otto is a fleeting bee. Besides, I spent one Christmas holiday alone in a relative's home while they were out of town and finished up a book during that time. Sure, I drank a lot of wine and spent a lot of time in anxiety spirals, but I produced something which has in turn released a lot of serotonin hits for me. Getting things published gives me happiness, makes me feel high. And it's all in my power. The sensation of chasing achievements is something I globbed onto in the aftermath of substance abuse times. My self-medication times. As soon as I started medicating myself to deal with feeling alone, even though certain people didn't take responsibility for betraying me, I *had* to take responsibility for my actions. It was as if everything before canceled itself out. Because I became an addict and all the stereotypes and archetypes of addicts — she has to take responsibility for her actions, only she can help herself, addicts can't be trusted, addicts are liars, addicts have no soul — all the goodness I'd possessed previously was void, vanished. I could never be trusted with money again because I was an addict, despite never stealing and barely lying. The most lying I did was lying by omission, hiding how bad my self-medicating had become. So taking control of my life, proving that I was in fact trustworthy and stable, led me in part to become such a workaholic. I could replace cocaine with achievements. Snorting achievements.

All that being said, writing went just about as well as expected this Christmas Eve evening: lots of anxiety spirals, not so much productivity, which stings even more when you promise yourself you'll be productive on a holiday.

Well, I may as well get some dinner. And *what* a dinner I should have, I thought.

I thought about Krystal's description of the sea urchin spaghetti.

That is where I shall go, I told myself.

I walked the dark alley up to the restaurant, a red door stood surrounded by cobblestone and reflective lights. But like before, it was closed. I retreated and walked into a square, passing a sandwich board menu written in English. It's for tourists, I noted. My eyes scanned the list. Spaghetti for 24 euros seemed higher than other places, but they had sea urchin spaghetti.

I sat at a table with a red tablecloth and an extra layer of brown paper covering the top, a single red Christmas candle in the middle, half burned down. The sea urchin pasta didn't disappoint; salty and satisfying. I drank wine and stared at my Kindle, trying to soak in words but they weren't sticking. I awkwardly tried to get the check so I could go back to my place and stare at screens in private.

That hole-filled eve, I spent a lot of time staring at my computer, staring behind my computer, staring at the wall, the ceiling, feeling the urge to jump out of my skin. I kept thinking: what *did* I want to write about? My mind kept wandering back to me and my agent's breakup. *She's not waiting on me for any new material. I have no books coming out soon so there are no publishers waiting on anything. My Submitttable is full of rejections; no literary magazines want my stuff. You focus so much on career, but it's not even going well. You're gonna die and this will all be for nothing.*

Write for you, I told myself. Write for you. Because you like it. You *do* like it.

I had plenty I wanted to write about, new stuff. But shouldn't I complete all my unfinished projects first? What about that goddamn memoir about high school my agent was trying to pitch around, about the time I was accused of wanting to shoot up my school; more specifically, the time people thought I was going to murder Chinga, along with other classmates, because I'd written a joke story in which he and other kids from my school died. I should try to find a home for that, right? It's important. Or does it not matter at all? Would it look pathetic if I sent query letters to agents on Christmas Eve? I mean, how pitiful, right?

I put on the 1985 freestyle song "Maria Magdalena," by the German synthpop group Sandra. In the 80s and early 90s, with the help of her then-husband and musical partner, Michael Cretu. During a brief height of popularity, she outsold Madonna in a number of countries around the world.

"*You take my love*
*You want my soul*

*I would be crazy to share your life*
*Why can't you see what I am*
*Sharpen your senses and turn the knife*

*Hurt me and you'll understand*
*I'll never be Maria Magdalena.*"

I kept playing it, it just felt like such a bright and sparkly song, like glitter raining down from a lonely overpass frequented by truckers and serial killers in the middle of the night,.

I'd write a few words then dip back out and doom scroll, trapped in my usual social media trap: check all 7,238 of my apps and dating sites then go back in. The obsessive checking of this unimportant garbage was slowing down my productivity.

And wasn't that all life was about, productivity?

I thought about how Kyle told me I had to chill out about that. I did. I knew I did.

You have no hobbies, he'd tell me.
I do, I'd say. Writing. Writing is my hobby.
That's not your hobby, he'd tell me. That's your career.
He wasn't wrong.

Well, I'd say, I write things on the side of my career. There's my day job writing and then the other writing I do, and when I don't work on that, I read, so I can be a better writer. When we lived together I was in school full time, also for writing, while working full time as a writer and trying to get books published.

"I guess my hobby is watching reality TV," I told him. He rolled his eyes.

I then thought about when the cast of *Jersey Shore* when to Italy. Being Italian was one of their main identities, yet when they got to Italy, they could not communicate with people. More than that, their loud and brash presence irritated the locals. So much so that the mayor of Florence banned the cast from numerous establishments. I laughed.

I went into the kitchen and fixed myself another drink: poured wine to the rim of a tall glass. I drank and listened to 10cc's "I'm Not In Love" on my headphones until I felt dizzy and had to lay down. Soon enough I felt tears rolling down my cheeks. Just this time last year, I felt like I had family. Sure, I was waiting for that stupid ring to make that officially true, but we were at his mom's large house in rural Massachusetts sprawled out on extra large couches and recliners, wearing matching pajama sets and covered in fleece blankets.

When we broke up, I told him it felt so good to feel folded into a family again, like a warm blanket soaking up my spilled self. I told him I was scared to lose it. I said that I was going to miss his mom and he said she wasn't going anywhere. I told him that I couldn't spend holidays with her anymore without looking insane.

"Anyway, you have plenty of friends," he said. "You'll be fine."

I resented him. I resented him for having a mother who still hosted Christmases and still bugged him to come home for holidays, a mother he'd often neglect, in my opinion. I'd remind him to buy her flowers or a card for Mother's Day and he wouldn't. I should have known, I told myself, I should have fucking known not to date him. My mother always said that clues for how a man will treat you are in how they treat their own mothers.

"You can still talk to her," he told me, when I cried about losing his mom through the breakup.

"It's not the same," I said. "You know it won't be the same."

He continued to assure me that I had plenty of friends and I'd be fine. That I had my career. But I told him those were two different things. I wanted family. It was more cemented, not as floaty. He looked at me like I was nuts.

I put on "Grooveline" by Heatwave, a disco pop hit my mom used to play on her record player all the time. I took a deep breath in, thinking about how it was hard to miss her, how to quantify it. She felt, at times, like a high school or college friend whom I'd lost contact with. She was 20 when I died, so did I really know her at all? Did I know Kyle's mom more in some ways? At the very least, she saw the woman I became. My mom only saw me as a kid, a kid she'd take for a vanilla shake at McDonald's anytime I had a doctor's appointment, or when I got my wisdom teeth out. How I wished I could go back in time for real by just sucking on one of those shakes.

$

The day after Christmas, I shopped. I went in and out of department stores and little boutiques on all the touristy streets. I tried on hats. I felt silk, cotton, and fleece in between my fingers. It felt like home.

It felt like drugs.

I bought some fuzzy zip up with a Minnie Mouse logo and ears on the hoodie part, of all things, it just seemed the warmest. I also bought a cheap striped sweater. I had underestimated how chilly it could be here. It reminded me of when I visited San Francisco for the first time; I only brought shorts and tank tops since it was always hot and sunny in California in my mind.

I bought a velvet blazer, made in Italy, from a vintage store. It was red and black and kind of reminds me of a Hugh Hefner jacket and these green velvet shorts with a thick black button in the middle. I shopped for hours trying to find a good pair of Italian leather boots. All the boots were made in China, at least where I was looking. I did find a pair of Italian made leather platform shoes but boots, not so much.

I also tried to find the perfect Italian leather purse. I must have spent an hour searching for one this day. Sure I'd find Italian brands but they were big brands like Dolce and Gabbana. I wanted something more unique. I found a leather shop where Krystal had happily got herself a bag on a whim, but I couldn't decide on one I wanted. I just wasn't satisfied with anything. Maybe it was because I was shopping alone. I think if I had someone with me, I'd buy something because they would be attached or stuck to the item somehow, but by myself it all seemed meaningless, like if I just fucked a bunch of Tinder dudes in speedos. Nothing. Nothing I liked.

✝

"Do you think you will ever write about me?" Otto asked while we embraced underneath his hand painted ceiling. The mural was from the 1800s. I told him it looked like it belonged in a museum. He said that was an American thing to say.

I laughed, feeling tingly in my fingers and where his body was pressing against me.

"If I do, it won't be good," I said with a smirk.

I grabbed another cookie from the night table beside his bed. Amelia watched me with envy.

"Thank you again for these," referring to the half-eaten gingerbread man in my hand, home baked and painted by his mother in Bavaria. "I feel bad I didn't get you anything."

"I never get anything for anyone or do anything for anyone out of obligation," he said. "Just because I want to."

I smiled.

He logged into a streaming service and we skimmed past a thumbnail for *Diehard*.

I laughed.

"In American movies, Germans are often the villains so who are the standard villains in German movies? I asked. "Americans?"

He scoffed and told me that was an American thing to say.

"Yeah but what's the answer?"

He didn't answer.

"When's your brother coming?"

"In the morning, around ten," I yawned. "I'm gonna pick him up before work."

Hours later, my brother was making "New Year, New Me!" jokes as we walked the cobblestone streets.

"My New Year's resolutions are to be more reckless with my body, work out less, and vow to never see a therapist, ever, like my ex said," I exclaimed, giggling.

I looked at my phone.

"Otto says we have to all buy red underwear too, some kind of tradition."

We went into a Yamamay, a lingerie chain.

"A lingerie shop isn't exactly the ideal place to be with my sister," my brother uncomfortably remarked.

Still, we both bought red underwear, for the sake of the new year. I secretly hoped that the new year could bring a change. I would find a way to make there be change, positive change.

On the way back, we walked by a corner clothing store, a next-door neighbor to the deep-fried fish store. One jumpsuit caught my eye, literally, the sequins caught the sun and reflected into my eyes. *This* was what I wanted, tacky and cheap, no doubt, but I loved it. My brother saw me checking it out and echoed my thoughts, "Cool Eurotrash look."

I swiped it up. Next thing I was curling my then-dark curls, standing in front of my bedroom mirror, the place feeling as sparkly as the glittery top of my outfit. It was nice having my brother there, who was in the bathroom singing while getting ready. Things felt more vibrant with him around.

Buzz.

Otto was at the door wearing cowboy boots, a western shirt, and black leather pants with a black leather belt.

"Are you sure you're not gay?" my brother asked with a laugh (my brother is gay). He was immediately comfortable being brash with him.

"Oh shut up," Otto said with a laugh, pushing his gray hair behind his ear.

We started walking down the stairs. "We walking?' Matt asked.

"It's just like a 25 minute walk."

We headed out with Matt chiming, "I wish we could get an Uber."

"You Americans and your Ubers."

As we walked block after block, explosions went off all around us. Suddenly I heard a hissing sound and there was a red stick right by my foot, with a fire going down the wick, like a cartoon stick of dynamite. My brother and I screamed. I kicked it and it blew up in the street.

Otto laughed.

"Dude, this is insane," I said, as other blasts continued to go off, both in the sky and spots on the ground all around us. I began laughing. "This is absolutely wild."

Soon we were at the entrance at Cattedrale di Palermo, a castle-like cathedral surrounded with the kind of tops I'd draw as a kid when instructed to draw a castle, flat-ish with dozens of pointed grooves, good for warding away dragons. It featured a threatening looking clock tower, a Mosque-looking rotund top-section, as well as four towers and two arches.

"This was built in the 1100s," Otto said. "You can really see the melting pot of all the influences. Some Arab, some Greek, Baroque even."

There was a large courtyard filled with shrubs, palm trees, and open space in front of the monstrous, majestic building. It was surrounded by gates. Some teens were climbing up them, throwing fireworks onto the property.

"Otto!" a man yelled from a balcony directly across from the castle. It was a slender man, seemingly in his mid-thirties, wearing fitted black jeans and a gray knit sweater, similar to what a fisherman would wear, only in Italia turtleneck form. He had a firecracker in his hand. He lit it and threw it at the ground.

"Una momenta," he said, and went inside.

We walked toward the door and waited a bit as firecrackers continued to explode around us. The man let us in, kissed us all on the cheeks, and led us into his home. The apartment looked like another smaller version of a castle to me. Each room was at least 60 feet wide, some with checkerboard floors like a giant chess board and roses painted on ceilings. There must have been sixteen rooms, most of which had no furniture. We walked into one room featuring a solo red balloon on a Victorian looking velvet chair. I remember thinking that the scene would be suitable for a gorgeous portrait with the proper subject. I didn't feel like that subject at this particular moment.

In the kitchen there were trays of pasta, seafood, and chips. We drank and ate and held sparklers and my brother and I marveled at how big the space was while Otto and his friends talked in Italian.

At some point, we posed for pictures. There is a photo of Otto and me in a window archway, at almost the peak of our affair. He has his right arm around me, touching my left wrist lovingly as I play with some bottom strands of my hair. I'm looking at him with adoration, as if I truly was in love with him at that moment. As if I would have willingly jumped into the rabbit hole of love and let him lasso me in. Every photo of myself I tried to get taken that night, I felt like I looked bloated and strange. I wanted my signature blonde hair back. It seemed my hair had dulled me, plus the roots were coming on it.

Otto took me and my brother to a cramped little punk rock bar, not far from Teatro Massimo after the party. I looked over at my brother wearing a solemn expression. I grew worried he felt like a third wheel or that everyone was in a relationship but him.

Tipsy, I found a way to swim through the crowd shelled in leather jackets and scarves to order us all a drink. I got a vodka tonic for Matt and myself. Otto didn't want a drink.

"You doing okay?" I asked Matt.

"Yeah, yeah," he nodded.

The drink pushed me slightly over the edge. I was enjoying the music, some Sicilian "trash" music as Otto had explained.

I began swaying to it.

"Do not you dance?" Otto asked.

"I am." I sipped my drink, rotating lights from the ceiling swirled in the plastic cup, turning it into a kaleidoscope. "I'm not much of a dancer. Never have been."

"Dance with me."

I felt uncomfortable. I just hugged him closer, swaying slightly.

"I'm gonna go check out the gay club up the street," my brother said.

"Are you sure? I'm sorry if we're being annoying."

"Yeah, you're good." He left.

"Please dance with me," Otto pleaded.

I closed my eyes and felt the music and the alcohol and tried to follow Otto's movements. I felt like the sparkler I'd held an hour before, like I was flying far away from the world I was born in. Fuzzy, almost like I was on molly. We kissed and it felt extra sparkly, as sparkly as the sequins on my pants suit rubbing up against Otto.

"Ow, one of your sequins scratched up my arm." He retracted his arm and rubbed where the short sleeve touched the skin.

The music died out like a short fuse. The lights went on and we went out to the street to search for my brother. We found him in front of a bar and I handed him the keys to my place, telling him I'd be over early so we could explore. He hugged us.

"Later, have fun with the German Chinga," he said as Otto and I walked toward his place.

I shuddered.

"What does that mean?" Otto asked.

"It doesn't matter. Inside joke. He's just kind of being a jerk." I said with a nervous laugh.

The two didn't look the same, but I could see *some* resemblance now. Aren't we just attracted to the same person over and over?

We waddled back past Teatro Massimo. Couples hung on the gates of the theater, holding bottles of champagne. We walked down via Cavour and down to the pizza shop that I now associated with the gateway to his home. A man was standing on the street selling hot steaming sfincione squares.

"Oooh, I want to get one." I reached for two euros out of my back pocket.

"Grazie mille."

Otto imitated my American accent by mimicking, parroting, echoing my "grazie millie."

"Oh stop it, why don't ya?" I said in an Italian accent while shaking my hand in a very Italian manner. "Que scifo!"

"See that's better! That sounds legitimate."

"But I'm just fooling around. You don't think it looks like I'm mocking them?"

"No you gotta act."

I thought of a friend who said he completely changed his persona when he was in Germany; he said it helped him to speak the language. He became angrier, more animated. He said it was effective. Maybe I just have to put on the mask. That's how you can become acclimated. That's how you can become respectable.

❢

In Otto's bed under a painted ceiling once again, but surrounded in sequins and leftover New Year's Eve glitter, I stretched out, put on my clothes and kissed Otto bye.

"Ciao," he whispered after lips went smack.

I returned to my place, where my brother was sleeping in my bed. I showered and hummed the "Despacito" song. Then I began singing it in the way Kyle and I used to sing basically every song.

"Don't you want to bucky bucky buck buck bito, I want to bucky buck buckasito," I sang as I brushed my hair in the bathroom. I blackened my pale eyelashes, filled in my eyebrows, and crammed black liner onto my top lids. I felt alive with another person in my place, in my space, in a pleasant way.

"Amelia," my brother said in a sing-song voice from the other room. He was awake.

"Hey Matt, you wanna go get a coffee?"

"Definitely."

I thought about bringing up the "German Chinga" comment but figured, nah, why stir the pot. I didn't want to be reminded of any painful patterns I was guilty of anyhow.

"I want an iced coffee," he told me, putting a coat on over his clothes. I zipped up my own.

"Oh trust me, I'd love nothing more than that. But they don't really *do* iced coffees here. Or in Europe in general."

"Ugh. What about just a drip coffee."

"Hmm.. We could walk up to Ruggerio Settimo Street. I bet that some of the more touristy shops have that."

"How much of a walk is that?"

"Hmm like a mile."

"Ugh."

"Yeah. I know I wish we could call a fucking Lyft or Uber."

Want and can are two different things, though. So we trekked our hungover asses, Amelia in tow, on this first day of 2019 to find the American drip coffee our patriotic selves desired so desperately. We walked and walked. The cool sunshine hit my cheeks. We passed crowds wearing all black, teens with curly hair giggling and chattering in Italian, and the occasional blonde tourist holding hands with another of the same hair pigmentation.

"How much longer?" Matt asked. We passed numerous cafes that were genuinely Italian and displayed an array of pastries. They, however, only made hot cappuccinos and espressos. Drip coffee was a total sin.

Bing. Bing.

Texts from Otto asking what we were doing.

"I can show you two around."

"Nah gonna have a bit of sibling time."

" 😟 "

"How about tomorrow?"

Sure I didn't know as much about the area as Otto but I didn't want him to take our quality time hostage.

Though my brother also had dating on the mind. He was chatting with some dudes on dating apps, prepping to make plans for that eve. He agreed to meet up with one, so I told him to have a good time and that I'd spend the night writing. I ended up drinking and chatting with some friends on Messenger instead.

"What a fun and exciting life you lead," one said. "I'm so jealous."

But I was jealous of the stability of their life. Being able to come home to a partner.

The next morning, I woke to the buzzing of my apartment door.

I pressed parlé, "Ciao?"

"It's me," my brother said groggily.

He came back looking recoiled, disturbed.

"How was the date, Matt?"

Looking mildly traumatized, he said, "He kept saying 'I love you.'"

"Oh dear god, they're all like this here!"

My brother dropped his backpack on the ground and plopped onto the couch.

I sat down next to him. "What happened? Where did you guys go?"

He rubbed his eyes with his hands.

"I don't want to talk about it."

He changed the subject. "Are you really staying an extra month to hang out with your new boyfriend here?"

"Well, yes and no." I went to the cupboard to get myself a glass. "You want one?"

He nodded affirmatively.

"He's not my boyfriend. And partially, yes, it's nice to have someone here, but also I thought I'd know where I'd want to move in the States by now. I think I need another month to figure it all out."

I'd booked another month in Palermo, requesting one more month in the same place. I figured I could enjoy another month of amazing food. And sure, I also wanted to see where things could go with Otto.

The night after my brother left town, Otto came over for a sleepover party. He introduced me to a German movie he liked as a kid, a coming-of-age story about a boy in West Berlin as the wall was coming down.

After the movie, we played around with each other's bodies for hours.

With arms intertwined, he asked if my last name was really Tron.

"It is now. When the reboot of *Tron* had just come out. I changed my Facebook name from Conn to Tron. Then it became my pen name. Then I really liked it, and later, out of spite, I changed it legally because a newspaper wouldn't let me use my pen name. So, I just had it changed."

"How American to name yourself after a movie."

"Yeah, I guess," I moved his arm off my shoulder so I could adjust my body more comfortably to his.

"I never even watched *Tron*," I added.

"Which one?"

"Either." I turned off the bedside lamp and everything went black. There were no windows to let in any light, after all.

"You named yourself after a movie you didn't even watch?"

I didn't tell him the *real* reason I picked it. It was the aftermath of the rape incident. Yeah, I couldn't tell you if it was late 2010 or early 2011 that I changed it, but it was because I was worried about the rapist finding me on Facebook. The movie *Tron* was out and Tron and Conn rhymed, so I just picked that, on a whim really. There was no meaning behind it. It's funny how something so meaningless at the time is now my fucking name. If I had known that would happen, I would've put more thought into the letters in it, but I think it's fine. I guess there's some poetry in it all too — not so much that the rape itself changed me, but that I became more robotic, more distant in its aftermath, particularly with interpersonal relationships. The name literally cut me from family ties as I was making the effort to cut myself emotionally from them, never to be hurt again. I never got as close with people as I did before. I could get closer to people I slept with, if I liked them enough, as I keep saying, but even in those scenarios I began to wear armor. Even if we weren't using condoms.

But Otto and I always used condoms. The one time I hinted that we didn't, he was horrified.

"You can get pregnant that way, or worse."

I had the sudden desire to call him a narc, even though he was obviously right.

When we woke up, he asked me if I wanted to get an arancina and go to the park.

I said that would be awesome. We wandered down the road with Amelia to a shop where arancine were just two euros apiece and got one each and a cassata to share.

We walked past a turtle pond under palm trees and sat on a bench nearby bushes of tropical flowers. In front of us a pink dome looked like some sort of stage. The inside of it, just like Otto's ceiling, was hand-painted art.

I felt elated sitting next to him on the bench, enjoying the savory ragu and cheese inside the deep-fried ball, recalling his insides oozing out of him just hours before. I was starting to feel comfortable in my own skin, and while I wasn't in a relationship, technically, it was the closest to feeling sexy in a situationship since my breakup, honestly since the beginning of me and Kyle's relationship.

"I really enjoy fucking you." I hovered my right hand over his and squeezed it flirtingly.

"Can you ever just be quiet?!" he snapped. "Sometimes it's good just to enjoy the atmosphere around you."

Almost instantly my eyes welled up with tears. I'm not the biggest crier, but I can rain easily if I feel rejected by someone I like, someone I'm fucking. This felt like all the months of sexual rejection I felt from Kyle were just pouring out of my pores.

"Sometimes it's just good to be quiet. We don't have to talk all the time."

He then saw how upset I was. "I'm sorry, hey, I just don't want to talk all the time."

He caressed my hair, gently.

I suddenly felt as alone as when I walked down the vicolo to my first place. Unknown and scary. I wanted to run, and simultaneously wanted to snap at him, but didn't. Don't do what you did with Kyle or some of the others you weren't dating as seriously, I reminded myself. Don't lash out. You'll only end up with more regret. Instead I sat sullenly and tried not to cry-cry.

He picked a red, tropical-looking flower from a nearby bush and put it in my hair. I smiled but it was forced.

"Well I should get back home. I do have to work in like an hour." It was nearly noon.

"Okay." He kissed me goodbye and I walked into the decrepit cement alley, which smelt like particularly strong piss today and was filled with cat feces on a mound of sand which came from God knows where. I walked past the religious statue nestled in the hole in the cement, surrounded by its corroding wall and scowled at it.

I smiled at the grocery worker who was always outside the store by my building while I pressed the code. I hopped in the shower and stood in the hot water until it ran out. It must have been about 10 minutes and I didn't even use any soap.

I got out of the shower, toweled off, and sent him a message on WhatsApp, thinking to myself, *don't be mean, but communicate how you feel*.

"You really hurt my feelings today. It felt like a rejection because I was talking about something sexual."

I didn't mention my past with Kyle.

"We were in a public place. I don't want people to hear that," he wrote back. "But it wasn't rejection."

I suddenly felt a very strong force inside me telling me not to try anything sexual with him again.

"I'll let him do that, initiate," I said aloud. "If I even want to."

My stomach was starting to growl. The window, once sunny, was now dark.

I ordered delivery from the seafood place from Christmas Eve. I got some pasta and two orders of sarde a beccafico: sardines stuffed with raisins and pine nuts, rolled up and baked in between fresh bay leaves.

Then I finished watching *Surviving R. Kelly* to start my workday, so I could write about his and Aliyah's relationship:

*Kelly met Aaliyah when she was just 12. He was introduced to her through Barry Hankerson, her uncle and his manager. Kelly and his team then took her under their (arguably creepy) wings as she began her recording career.*


I reflected as a woman in her thirties on Aaliyah, a woman who was older than me by a few years when she blew up. A woman who was so adult before she even grew up and only 22 when she died. If I died at 22, I wouldn't have even had the chance to mature. I was dating such losers at that time, whom I've since had time and space to process. She never had the chance to process who and what she dated. She never had the chance to process that she was likely groomed and abused by an adult man when she was just a child.

My annoyance and confusion subsided less than twenty-four hours later, after Otto sent me links to different music videos over Facebook chat. When friends and acquaintances sent me music videos I would feel this pull, this weight, a block thrown upon my stomach. It was time consuming, something I had to do and spend my time on and then give feedback on. It was like being asked to critique someone's twelve-page essay or something. I felt guilty for being annoyed by people's attempts to connect with me. It all felt so draining. But from Otto, I craved it. Why? Because I was touching his dick, I suppose. Because I liked him and was fucking him.

"I am going to tell you something that people say here: *Ti voglio bene*" he wrote with a heart emoji.

I Put it into Google translate. The phrase translated to "I love you" in English.

Oh god. I felt queasy. I felt equally drawn to and disgusted by his confession of love. Then I got another notification.

"Don't worry. It's not the same as Te Amo."

There are two types of love, he explained, though sometimes they can overlap a bit. He said Te Amo is romantic love while Ti Voglio Bene can be for friends but also family and lovers.

"Huh. Americans, we need this," I wrote back, feeling mildly disappointed. "We also need different versions of the word friend. One for the kind of friend who doesn't know your last name and then for the kind of friend who you have been intimate with, and then yet another for some of the gradients in between. I know there's fuck friend, best friend, good friend, great friend, a friend, but I don't know, all those words minus fuck friend are kind of vague. Best friend I guess implies top tier friend but there's something so middle school about it."

"You're a weirdo," he wrote back. "Anyway, I'm gonna get ready. I'll see you soon."

Heart emoji.

It was a rainy night, one of the first rainy nights I went out since arriving. I went to the local dollar store to pick up an umbrella. While there were plain black ones, simple and sleek and perfect for Italian style, I opted for tacky and childish: a literal children's umbrella covered with images of penguins.

Otto had asked me to meet him at the "piazza with all the statues," closest to my old apartment. I walked toward the plaza through the dark streets, now glossy from sprinkles of rain, holding my new baby umbrella above my head to avoid hair frizz and leaky mascara. I noticed how quiet and still the city felt. Except for the rhythmic pitter patter of the rain. Except the rhythmic sound of car engines in unison. And then, the sound of one engine closer than the rest, slowing down, a car, creeping up to me. I saw its upper right tire rolling beside me first, quietly, slowly, *stalking*. Then, the sound of a car's automatic window rolling down.

The driver, the only person in the car, yelled something at me as I continued to walk. The car kept rolling slowly beside me. My eyes darted around the area, nobody else was around, just some lights above. I was in the dark zone, the area between my palace and the area I used to live, with less activity at night, darker buildings, more run-down vibes as the locals would call it.

The man continued to try to speak to me in Italian. I turned, to see him with one hand on the steering wheel, his body craned towards me. He was middle aged with a scruffy beard.

"No parlo Italiano."

"Want a ride?"

"No capito," I mumbled, eyes forward.

My heart began beating, the pretty rain sounds warped into bleak memory.

"Ride. I'll give you ride."

"No grazie," I said coldly and kept walking.

The tires began moving faster, less-predator-like, and he drove off into the darkness. I let out a deep breath of relief, but suddenly the world around me seemed much more antagonistic.

All the dark stairways and alleys ahead and behind me, all the storefronts now closed, felt like dark holes for monsters to fester in. When I was a child, I'd tell my parents that I could see semi-transparent creatures coming out of the dark holes of the radiator. I named them frickles.

A few blocks later, and the light of the more touristy area ahead was shining like a star. My breathing calmed, my gait slowed, but I felt colder. And then, standing under white Christmas lights in the piazza, stood Otto wearing a plaid scarf, applying chapstick. I ran up and hugged him.

"Some dude tried to pick me up in his car."

He laughed. "Yeah, that area is a bit run down. A lot of sex workers."

My heart was beating slower now that I wasn't alone, physically. "How far is your friend's place?"

We were going to a small, intimate party held by one of his long-time friends.

"About an hour walk."

*Jesus Christ.*

"But we can take this bus partially there." He led me to a bus stop just a few feet away.

"Do we need passes?"

"No, that and the schedule are never clear. Italians! It's chaos."

He grabbed hold of my umbrella and pulled it toward him to examine the top.

"Why did you buy a child's umbrella?"

I shrugged, "Thought it was cute." I looked at the cartoon character on it and his smile. I smiled just at the sight of it.

No sooner than five minutes later, the bus arrived. We climbed in and about ten minutes later were off, standing on a fancy street with a closed Gucci shop. Our walking trip commenced.

"They don't get kitsch here, you know," Otto continued, looking at my umbrella. "It's not like Germany and America.

They'll just think there's something wrong with your brain here. It's only children and adults here. No irony. You're living in the purgatory zone if you continue this way, unable to fully connect with the locals."

Otto held my hand as we walked. The air felt colder and colder.

"My tutor said I'm getting better," I told him.

"I think you are slow at learning other languages."

"I mean definitely, it's one of my worst flaws. That's why I got her!"

The rain felt icy, a familiar feeling and smell.

"What!?" I yelped at the sight of white balls falling.

"Oh my god," Otto said. "I've never seen snow here."

At Otto's friend's place we sat on pillows on the ground surrounded by art. One woman showed me some handmade tarot cards she'd made, then we played a game with some other cards of her creation, animal-based. It was more of an astrological reading than a game I guess. I think I picked the snake.

Otto talked in Italian with his friends, before turning to me and saying, "Oh we are reflecting about a girl I had a story with in Sardinia."

"Have a story?" I asked.

"Sorry, that's just what people say here, for like, relationships. Or, not even relationship, dating."

I repeated the phrase in my head. "I like it. It sounds nice. Better than other phrases, I suppose. Like hooking up. I'm learning so much today."

When the evening was done my legs were tired. I stood wobbling at my apartment building's doorway with Otto towering over me.

"Do you want to come in?"

He told me he wanted to sleep at home that night. Feeling a little rejected, I smiled, "Okay, well, get home safe."

Then he kissed me and stared at me with a look that I knew well, the look of a man who thought he was in love with me. He then confirmed my suspicion.

"Gina, I, I think men fall in love with you very easily."

Okay, this meant the Te Amo way for sure. My cheeks got hot and I shrugged, grinning. I struggled to find something to say, something sweet but not too sweet and certainly nothing vulnerable.

"It's been known to happen," is what I came up with.

He responded shyly, "I know that is what happened to me."

Scared, I didn't reciprocate verbally but kissed him back.

"Sure you don't want to come in?"

He nodded.

I went inside the warm building, feeling frosty at the tip of my nose and disoriented by the evening's unfoldings. This is great, I thought, closing my umbrella and walking up the stairs.

I was welcomed by Amelia jumping on my calves. I reached down to pet and accept kisses. She likely had to pee. I thought of the man who pulled his car over earlier. The dark outside became an abyss I dreaded meeting. With my coat still on, I latched her up and brought her back downstairs. I "walked" in front of the door of my building, the only spot covered in harsh light. There were demons living in the shadows. The dark parking lot filled with parked cars seemed humanless, but who knew who or what was sleeping in the cars, under them, slithering under rocks like snakes.

The next morning, I woke feeling guilty I didn't tell Otto I was falling in love with him. Perhaps he felt rejected? Was I falling in love with him though? I certainly wasn't *in* love with him, but could see it approaching if it all kept up. I certainly felt some explosions with him. But I also felt explosive. I figured I'd let him know I felt similar. As promised, there is no love in this story. I did not actually fall in love with him nor was I planning to tell him so. But it felt like, just as with Kyle and marriage, things were inching toward it. The love was visible, like the sun in the distance when you walk down a hill. By the time you get close enough to feel it, it sets.

Otto suggested we have a "Palermo night on the town." Still aglow from his profession of lovey feelings, I happily obliged.

We started with an aperitivo, which for most bars meant buffet-style homemade treats in addition to marked down drinks. We strolled slim thoroughfares through mortar and concrete plastered with bubbly neon graffiti, subdued murals of roses, and white cursive Italian script. I walked carefully over the cobblestones, trying to avoid lodging my boot toe in a crevice and falling on my face.

We returned to the establishment where our first date took place. It was much busier so the river view window was barely visible. A rockabilly band stood in front of it, a few men in black and white striped shirts and a woman wearing a black halter with black jeans.

The crowd kept swelling until Otto's thighs were pushed against my own, his warm breath like a dewy cloud around my nostrils, a familiar animal scent.

"Dance with me," he demanded. *Ugh.* I'd been dreading the possibility as soon as we'd stepped in the door.

I could not. I wasn't drunk enough, or into the music enough, and definitely didn't have enough room to dance. More than that, I was self-conscious. My tummy suddenly felt bloated, too big for my shirt. Also, I felt put on the spot.

I shrugged, "I can't right now," kissed his cheek and rubbed his upper torso lovingly.

He rolled his eyes. When they fell back in place, his pupils set on a woman to my right, dancing alone near the band. She had long, thick, blonde hair and an exposed collarbone. People started giving her room so she could freely flail her arms around as she moved her hips. I assumed she wasn't Sicilian, and liked her vibe, but wasn't appreciating the vibe I was picking up from Otto. I could almost sense him wishing he were with that woman, wishing he could go over and talk to her. Maybe he would. He did say that he "does what he wants to do" in life, that doing his own thing is his motto. The way he stared at her dancing made me feel like thousands of vases, under my eyes and in my throat, were breaking all at once. I fought the urge to run out of the club sobbing like a child. I wanted to lay in bed and cry like I did in junior high when others were coupling up and dancing, or like in high school when others were slow dancing at prom while I was banned due to writing about murder. I wanted to cry in bed like when Kyle no longer wanted to marry me, like I didn't measure up. Others were coupling up and I was not. They were slow dancing with significant others through various stages of their lives, watching their loves blossom like hydrangeas. I was continuously wilting. And writing. Often just writing about murder.

Maybe I never blossomed because my growth was stunted, possibly by my own doing. Maybe there was a break in the growth like a stick lodged in a plant trying to grow straight up, forcing it to grow sideways. I wanted to be able to dance, always have. I wanted to be normal. The first murder thing I ever wrote was the damn Elks' Club short story as a young teen, in which I accidentally murder Chinga. I wrote it years after getting upset about watching one of my friends slow dance with him. He knows this and we've never talked about it. Instead, we just moved across the country together years later without discussing any of it. Like normal people do.

"Otto," I kissed his cheek close to his ear, attempting to distract his gaze from the blonde. "Would you like anything from the bar?"

"No, thank you." He remained fixed on her hips.

I needed a strong drink to combat these feelings. It's a complex you have, I reminded myself. Get over it. Who cares if he's watching someone dance. Still, kinda shitty he's trying to force me to dance. Like I'm not fine as I am. Why can't anyone love me as I am?

It was stupid, but I'd hoped Otto could be different, despite the red flags waving around him. He was nothing more than a link in the chain I'd always followed, proof of that horrible old saying: wherever you go, there you are.

Soon, the dancing blonde left and Otto got tired - drained, he said - and we walked the two miles home. "God, I really wish we could get a damn taxi," I said. "Would make things much easier."

At my door, he kissed me.

"I'll come in tonight," he said. "I want to."

As we walked up the stairs, something in my brain told me I should reciprocate what he told me. Maybe that will fix his waning interest, his annoyance at me for not wanting to dance.

When we were making out in bed, I told him, "That thing you told me the other night, well, I been thinking about it and well, I think I am feeling the same way too."

It was dark except for the cool blue light of one of the cheap plastic lamps, but I saw him recoil like a snake, or a snail. He sat up and switched on the cheap plastic lamp by his side of the bed. I leaned over to him, while he sat in bed very poised. He suddenly looked like a grandpa or something. He was giving off big old man energy, plus another kind of energy I knew well, the energy of a man who was worried I wanted a relationship.

"I have been thinking too and I don't think I feel that way. Let's not go there. It's a bad idea."

We still had sex. After, I cried silently in the dark. I don't think Otto noticed.

My mind wandered back to a breakup about a decade earlier. I was visiting my boyfriend in Spain. It was my first trip to Europe. I was 26 and decided traveling abroad at least once before I died was worth going into major overdraft. There was a lot of crying and a lot of him yelling at me, but before all that, I felt disinterest, aloofness. as we explored Sevilla. It was another night in another European city, where the madness and chaos felt like it was coming only from us. Everyone around us would always be so jarringly calm.

"The American in me wants to see some violence once in a while," he told me. He had been living over there for months by that point. "Where are the fights over women? Women fighting over men? All the stuff I hate yet kind of want now because it feels like home? Simpsons references and bright box stores, which are the worst, but the cobblestones and romantic buildings just make me sick sometimes."

Romance, the idea of succumbing to it, while simultaneously finding myself incapable of doing so, was making me sick.

While Otto may have made it clear he didn't want a relationship, he sure as fuck texted like we were in one. All day.

"Good morning," he would text with a sun emoji and a kissy face emoji. It was starting to wear. No self-respecting man I'd fucked in America would ever send me heart emojis unless we were in a fucking relationship.

But seeing as this seemed to be the normal thing for the Europeans I was coming across, Italians in particular, I was trying to be open. I texted back a kissy heart face. It seemed inauthentic, especially since he'd been disturbed when I tried to reciprocate his love comment, but whatever. At least he wasn't mushy within three minutes of meeting me like the Italians. Try to stay open, and don't lash out, I reminded myself.

Then I received a text from a friend in Brooklyn. She was a nice person. I liked her. But the text tired me, drained me. Why didn't I like getting texts from her? Is it because I didn't like her as much as I thought? Where had all these friends come from?

God, it's so much energy to respond: How am I? How *am* I? What a question. What a *loaded* question.

But when I'd hear from Otto, it wouldn't be exhausting. It was a true treat to text back. My responses were elaborately detailed. Why him? He didn't deserve it. Was it just because I fucked him? This female friend, I've known for years. We'll likely be friends for much longer. Otto and I will likely be nothing in years. Why does my dumb brain want to pour so much concrete into our obviously wobbly structure?

Those let into my I-wanna-hear-from-you circle are few and far between. Sometimes it's hard to know why I let someone in. I will admit that a high percentage of this circle are people I have fucked, am fucking, or kind of want to fuck. Or truly love, I guess. Not everyone I've fucked is someone I want to hear from. Most of them, I don't, in fact.

Otto slept next to me, quietly and snoreless. My mind drifted to happy memories with exes. Even the worst one from my early twenties. Even the smelliest sewer has flower petals floating down the tunnels, maybe. This particular stinky stream had a whole lot, sometimes so much that it looked like a parade or a snake of cherry blossoms.

We'd laugh so hard together at television shows with our legs intertwined. We'd prank call people and I'd have to stuff my head under a pillow to stifle the chuckles. I thought my head would explode. There were times he rubbed my back in bed and caressed me until I fell asleep. He'd take me out for ice cream or Orange Julius under the giant orange bulb in Montreal. We'd lie in the shade of botanical gardens eating a seitan and cheese sandwich with lots of mustard, both of us wearing terry cloth shirts, perfect for cuddling. We'd kiss and hold hands. We'd laugh hysterically.

Another ex planted blooming kisses and proclamations while we snorted coke over a toilet. So many nights wrapped around each other or hitting each other consensually, admitting our darkest secrets to each other on borrowed time. While those timers have gone off and the memories and boys have dissipated, there was candy in it all.

"Why do you always have your passport on your table side? Just ready to go? What are you, a spy?" Otto asked, pulling his underwear up.

"You can use the shower if you want."

"Yes, I think I will do that."

"Okay, cool." I went to fetch him a towel.

"Well, hey, why don't we shower together?"

I hesitated to think about the lighting in the bathroom. It was bright, the type of fluorescent that betrays days of bad acne and adds a particular luster to breast cancer scars.

"I don't know."

"Why not?" Otto begged. I handed him one of the towels my brother and I got ripped off for.

"Well, I don't know if I feel, I mean, I'm a little self-conscious."

"Of what?" he snarled.

I was wearing a thong and a t-shirt, so I just pointed to my chest area.

"Oh you are fine. I see you naked all the time."

I shrugged okay.

As we walked to the bathroom I began taking off my shirt, fearing the unforgiving light would smudge his perception of me.

We hopped into the stall.

"Nice zit."

A pesky whitehead was starting to spurt on my lower left cheek, a popular locale for the acne crowd.

"Thanks," I rolled my eyes, wishing I could glob some foundation over it, even in a shower full of steam. Hot water kept splashing my chest and bouncing up to my face, forcing me to squint. I reached for the soap caddy surrounding the shower head and clumsily bumped into Otto. Showering together is never as sexy as one imagines.

He kissed me anyway.

I felt a new sense of liberation. Here I was, completely naked in front of this man, with a non-concealed zit in horrible lighting and he still found me sexy. I felt my body shedding an invisible layer of filth accumulated since my cancer surgeries.

After we were clean, we walked with Amelia to get some arancini. On the way we saw a man beating his child with closed fists. People stood all around unphased. Half a block later, surrounded by palm trees, a woman yelled in our direction, "tuo cane ha bisogno di un cappotto."

"Huh?"

"She's saying your dog needs a coat," Otto mumbled.

# Eruptions

The word 'volcano' is derived from a small volcanic island in the Tyrrhenian Sea located about fifteen miles away from the island of Sicily. Its name is aptly Vulcano, and it's one of the seven Aeolian Islands, some of which are volcanic. I must admit I didn't know these islands even existed until Otto told me. I was instantly intrigued.

In order to get to them, we needed to take a train to the northern coastal town of Milazzo then catch a ferry to whichever island we wanted to visit. There were two that appealed to me: Vulcano, because duh, who wouldn't want to go to a tiny island home to an active and smoking volcano that birthed the very word! The other island I was drawn to was Stromboli. It's home to one of the world's most active and volatile volcanoes on earth. Around 300 people live right under it as it boils. Unlike Vulcano, it actually erupts, and you can climb to its top and peer inside. A dream, like walking into a National Geographic magazine.

But, it was off season. It was winter after all, despite it being around 60 to 70 degrees. I saw there weren't any tours scheduled but figured I'd email them just in case. They replied saying they did do solo tours but it would cost about $300. Otto told me it wasn't worth it. While he was concerned about the price, I was worried about being alone with some tour guide. What if they were a creep? What if they hit on me? What if I had to be alone in a car with them while my intuition went into panic mode? Not much of a vacation, huh.

"Gina, it's off-season. There won't be any visitors," Otto kept telling me, even about just visiting Vulcano, which had more available AirBnbs. And they were super cheap! Like twenty-five American bucks a night cheap.

"That's fine," I said, slipping into my bed in my new tiger pajama set. I pressed my back against his chest and crotch. As he put his arm over my side and snuggled up close, I added, "I don't need there to be other tourists, just as long as I can get food and write."

"I don't want to miss out on this opportunity," I told him. "I want to see real volcanoes."

"As you wish."

Oh. If I only understood how few people there would be.

Thinking about getting onto a train in a foreign country alone with a dog sounds stressful and scary even now. I get used to being around others. I don't like doing things alone. But I will if I have to.

With Amelia curled up in my lap, I watched sea waves crash upon rocks through the window of the train. We were the only ones in the car.

I pulled my Kindle out and continued reading *Brutally Honest*.

"You start to believe that it is you who is the crazy one because of all the times you feel you might be insane, you've got it all wrong, you don't know what you are doing, you don't know who to trust, who to like. You're the one who is responsible for being unhappy, for making him angry. You are the idiot, the slut, the bitch."

I put on "Too Much" by the Spice Girls and put on my earphones.

*"Too much of something is bad enough*
*But something's coming over me to make me wonder*
*Too much of nothing is just as tough*
*I need to know the way to feel to keep me satisfied "*

I was dreading trying to find a taxi at the train station. Otto told me cabs would be there, and that did make sense, but what if there weren't? Would I just have to walk? It looked far. What if the driver wouldn't let me in with a dog?

But he did.

"Italians, they love their dogs more than their people," I recalled Otto saying over and over.

Though it felt strange, I already knew I'd made the right decision when my speedy ferry boat, called a hydrofoil, bounced on the water. My Airbnb host said he'd pick me up. I knew he was likely safe, but was a little nervous. I thought back to how dumb people told me I was for getting into a car with a strange man, the man who ended up raping me. How was this different? Please don't be creepy. Please don't. I'm in the middle of the map, very very far away from anyone I love.

When the boat docked at Vulcano, I marveled at cliffs engulfed in seagulls flying in and out of sea mist. I felt like I was in some tropical movie, about to meet King Kong or dinosaurs.

There was the Airbnb host, a 50 to 60 year-old-ish man with smile lines in his face.

He seemed more like a grandpa than a rapist. And yes I know grandpas can be rapists, retired or working.

On the ride he tried to tell me where to buy what around town, but I was too transfixed on the smoking volcano. As we pulled into the driveway, it was just like the pictures of the place promised, I would have a full-on view of the volcano from my front door and patio. My cottage was right next door to the host's house, where he lived with his wife. Lemon trees and stunted palms divided the mommy home from its little daughter.

I entered the cottage, put down my bag, and reached for my phone in my purse.

Twenty minutes before work started. Damn, cutting it close. I pulled my laptop out of my bag and looked for wifi. I also searched around the kitchen nook and living room for a card or piece of paper which had the wifi name and password.

Nothing. It did say there was wifi in the listing. I'd made sure of it. I felt tension rising in my stomach, my shoulders, neck and hands. How the fuck was I going to work? I looked at my phone. Okay, 16 minutes before I had to start work. Why did I cut this so short? Why didn't I just take the fucking day off? The plan was to work from here, a break from the amazing but often crushingly claustrophobic Palermo.

I walked across the little courtyard, my laptop tucked under my right arm, and knocked on my host's door.

I smiled as best I could to mask the anxiety.

"Internet?" I asked.

"Quoi?"

I held up my laptop.

"Io lavoro," I said, choppily. Perhaps I just said "lavoro."

He nodded his head in recognition. He pointed at the guesthouse and shook his head no. I let out a sigh.

Then he motioned with his hand to follow him. He motioned to come in. I hesitated. I said in English, "Maybe I can get internet there," pointing to a plastic white lawn table sitting extra close to the house's patio doors.

I opened up my laptop and took a look. Yup, there was internet.

"Ok, buono, buono."

I sat on the table and the internet did indeed connect. Just not very well.

I was supposed to finish up a story about Ted Bundy and misogyny. I had pitched it following the release of *Conversations with A Killer: The Ted Bundy Tapes*, a docuseries I was asked to build stories around. I figured the answer was a clear yes, plus I could pull from Ann Rule's *The Stranger Beside Me*, one of the books that first got me into the true crime genre.

I had basically everything I needed to compile the article and finish it up. I had reached out to Dr. Diana York Blaine, the director of University of Southern California's Undergraduate Department of Gender and Sexuality, who asked me to send questions over email. I could just throw those into the article, some Ann Rule lines, some lines from the docuseries and I'd be golden.

I re-read Blaine's email. She said that in the United States, females are viewed as objects, "either exalted or degraded."

I paused and thought about that.

"Exalted or degraded," I whispered. A cool breeze blew past me and I looked up at the volcano smoking to my left.

I exhaled deeply.

I stated in my email to the expert that Bundy killed women while claiming to love *some chosen* women in his life, like his mom and girlfriend.

Re-reading her answer, which I'd only glazed over the other day, made the wind feel lonelier. She wrote that he "reflects a larger cultural belief that only certain females are worthy of men's love, that these women somehow transcend the stigmatized category into which we place 'woman.'"

She added that for men that see women this way, "there always lurks the possibility that the 'good' woman will become the 'bad' one, so misogyny is built into the system. This dual need to love and destroy suggests the precarity of normative masculinity."

Her comments jarred me. Because I knew they were real. Because some men in my past chose to see me as more bad leaning, for all sorts of reasons: because I dressed goth, because I did drugs, because I liked to hang out, because I didn't roll my badness into a ball and try to hide it in a crevice of my body. I wore it proudly instead. Men can be nuanced but women still can not, though that has been changing. Just not changing fast enough for my age group or my life. I've been a curious butterfly to follow, but when they follow you into a dark cave, it's your fault, despite not leading them there.

I tried to piece this together while continuously warming my hands. The sun started to set, casting a rainbow sherbet veil over the volcano. Grayish smokes plumed up the multi-color sky. When the gray and colors turned black, the host's wife came home, smelling like a strong, pink cloud of perfume. She was wearing bright red lipstick and told me I could come inside to warm up and write. But that seemed too imposing. Instead I roughed it, sitting at the plastic white table, soaking up the wifi from the house as the air turned more and more frigid.

I walked into my guesthouse to wrap my fuzzy Minnie hoodie around my shivering body and returned. Amelia stayed closer to me now, cuddling up to my ankles and staring at me in the manner which indicates she wants to be picked up and held in my lap.

I continued to work. While I was slightly uncomfortable, the air felt good, raw and fresh, far from pollution. I looked over to the shadow of the volcano beside me and breathed in. Just one more hour, then two days of writing my own stuff. I told myself it's even *better* that I don't have wifi in that little guest house. I can just focus on writing. I won't be distracted by the internet. I can just write poems inside the warmth of the little cottage.

After I filed all my stories, I figured I'd go walk downtown and grab something to eat. According to my phone, there was a restaurant open just at the end of the street. And it had outdoor seating in case they wouldn't let me bring the dog inside.

I leashed Amelia and we walked to the gate. I closed it and looked down the road, which looked much more terrifying than the morning my host picked me up and the sun was shining. It was so dark I couldn't see how far to the main road. I turned the flashlight of my phone on and began walking toward an abyss. On both sides of me were fences.

Suddenly, BANG! SNARL! YELP!

A growling beast of a dog was banging on chunks of plywood and fence to our right. I couldn't exactly see him but he sounded large and angry. I could see the wood rocking. My heart beat fast as we kept walking. Amelia calmed down after realizing there was no immediate threat.

Finally, we came to the end of that road. My GPS instructed to turn right.

I did so. It was all dark everywhere.

"You have reached your destination."

I lowered my phone's glaring light so my eyes could focus. When they did I saw a shut gate and a sad tiki bar in a very closed state. I sighed. In the distance I saw the light of what looked a convenience store.

I entered a very tiny shop that resembled a bakery but had only two items for sale, both pastries. I recognized one of them as a Baba, a penis-looking sponge cake soaked in rum. There were several bouncing around inside a container that held an ocean of rum. I purchased one and walked back past snarling dogs and darkness to the cottage. I devoured the cake, felt slightly drunk, and passed out.

I decided it would be better to venture around in the light.

Daylight came. It was an overcast Saturday, full of grays and void of work and snarling dogs. I walked to the miniature downtown, past stray cats crawling around green and blue human-made cat houses on the streets. Ahead of me, I saw hot springs. I could see a girl on her back soaking in the mud. I went to the gate but it wasn't open.

A car drove up beside me and the passenger window rolled down.

"Vuoi un passaggio?" asked a man, maybe in his late 50s or early 60s with gray hair and a striped shirt.

"No capito," I responded, ignoring him as I tried to figure out the hours on a white metal sign intertwined with the gate's metal.

"You want ride?"

"No grazie," I said, continuing to fiddle with the sign.

"I can give you ride."

"No," I said. "No grazie, No grazie."

He began to drive away then pulled off and stopped. Gas rose from the muffler like a snake. My entire body clenched until the car finally rolled out of sight. Suddenly I thought of an overpass, that damned overpass in Sunset Park, Brooklyn, long after the sun had sunk, running to it in my argyle dress, hoping I could find solace in a taxi, hoping he wasn't running after me but too scared to look back.

The girl in the mud somehow vanished from view, as if she'd been a mirage. I gave up trying to read the sign and continued traversing the tiny island. There was a cute little downtown, but every store seemed to be closed, the same for bars and restaurants. Finally, by the dock, I found a cafe. There weren't many options, just a few pastries. I ordered a cannoli and cappuccino and sat at a table under a big canopy. Taylor Dayne's "Tell it to my Heart" was playing.

A group of old men in newsie hats were at a table across from me playing some kind of card game. They gawked at me for a moment before loudly continuing their game.

When I went up to reconcile my food purchases, the young man at the register said, "You only tourist on island right now."

"Wow," I smiled. "Damn."

"Not good time," he said, gesturing outside. "Molto freddo."

Using my map app, I wandered down a desolate side road until it led to a beach with all-black sand. I crouched down to touch the little black pebbles. I took an empty water bottle from my bag and scooped up a few tablespoons worth. I stood and faced a rock formation in the distance, feeling the wind go through me. I wanted to linger and marvel but was completely alone on the beach. There was an industrial building nearby surrounded by fencing. A broken beer bottle stared up at me from the sand. It felt too isolated to relax. Seeing there was basically nothing to do, nobody to communicate with, I figured I'd go back to my place and write. On the way back, stray cats walked back and forth in front of me. One meowed. I could hear a car coming so I got out of the middle of the road. It started slowing down and I felt a sinking feeling.

It was that old man again, with his window down, again.

He offered me a ride again and I said no.

Looking dejected, he drove off.

Maybe he was just being friendly.

Or maybe he was a serial killer. At the very least, a serial rapist.

I wondered if there were any murderers on this island.

I wondered if there were any unsolved murders on the island.

Back at the cottage, I sat out on the deck and gazed in the direction of the smoking volcano. It was too dark to see the smoke.

I pulled out my phone, turned on the international plan and Googled "how many serial killers are there in Sicily?"

The first article was from the BBC in 2010.

*Italian police have arrested a 69-year-old man on suspicion of carrying out a series of murders in a town in Sicily. Giuseppe Raeli, who has no previous criminal record, has been charged with five murders and four attempted murders in Cassibile between 1998 and 2009.*

I looked down further.

"Meet the Sicilian Mafia Hitman Who Killed 80 People and Will Be Free in 5 Years"

Eh, a bit different.

I didn't bother to look up serial rapists in the area, because I knew very well that those existed everywhere. I imagined that the accurate number wouldn't be reported; I suppose the same goes with the United States. I closed my eyes and imagined bones buried just beyond the volcano, on the other side of the hill. I imagined corrupt cops not having the time to investigate, playing cards instead, gambling.

I sighed lying in bed listening to the thunder and snuggled close to Amelia with her sweet head resting on my forearm. Look at where I am now. Yes, in a cool place, but completely lonely. What is this all for?

Relax, Gina. Remember when you told yourself (several times) that you are once again, post-breakup, dedicating the rest of your life to becoming a crazy and deranged writer and not a wife? Well here we are, bitch! Here we mutherfucking are.

Be happy Gina, I told myself. David didn't care about your boob scars and neither does Otto. It wasn't the surgeries that made Kyle stop wanting to fuck you.

I scrolled my Facebook feed. Pic of couple kissing. Pic of college friend getting engaged. Meme about Mountain Dew. Then, a meme that said "You don't really want sex, you just want the physical validation that you are sexually desirable to replace the emotional rejection of being unlovable."

And so there it was.

I got a ding. Otto was asking how I was doing.

"Good, overall. But, some guy tried to get me to go into his car and I'm a little freaked out about it."

"You're not aggressive enough," he told me.

"Huh?"

"You need to be more aggressive!"

"Well, if I say no thanks and they go away, I think that is better than possibly escalating things."

"Fine," he wrote. "Then don't listen to me. I don't feel your response to these men is appropriate."

My heart started beating fast, like I was in one of my prior arguments with Kyle. It felt like there had been a pudding sculpture in there with Otto's name on it that was melting now, disintegrating.

"I am listening, I'm just saying that I would be scared to scream at someone who is possibly already considering getting sexual with me. Could end up in a bad situation."

He didn't respond.

Starting to feel butterflies in my stomach explode into vicious flying koalas, I angrily typed and sent: "You don't know what it's like to be a woman."

"Yeah, well men can also be assaulted," he wrote back.

My fingers started flying. "As for appropriate, I don't think your response to this situation is appropriate. I've been attacked before, and there was a car involved and the whole thing is very hard for me. Telling me what I should and shouldn't do when you aren't here, you don't know, I don't like that." Direct and to the point. I had to be assertive, but never mean. There. That's what I did. Right?

He didn't respond.

So I tried to call him. He didn't pick up. I began pacing around the tiny cottage, which now felt like it was caving in on itself. I could hear rain coming down outside.

"Can we talk about this? Maybe there is a misunderstanding," I texted.

Minutes passed like taffy being stretched. I opened the fridge and leaned on the door, peering into the all-white and nearly empty display. The only items in the fridge were a bottle of water and one leftover rum cake. I went over to the bed, fitted with the kind of multicolored comforter you'd find in a Florida beach house in the 1980s, and collapsed. I stared up at the ceiling and all its little bumps and scars. The rain was coming down harder now, and louder. I tried to enjoy its calming rhyme as I waited for the ding.

Ding.

"I think we should just be friends," wrote Otto. Thunder roared from outside in unison with the lightning urge to lash out.

"You really gonna break up with me over text?" I texted him.

"We aren't even in a story. So there is no break up. I just want to do what I enjoy and I do not enjoy this right now."

I rolled my eyes, turned my phone off, flicked off the light, and tried to fall asleep. But sleep I could not. I turned the light back on, stared at a crevice in the ceiling and sighed:

God, I hate myself.

I thought back to a conversation with my literary agent right before she dumped me mere days after Kyle. Then too, I felt I was just being assertive, honest, but not unreasonable or difficult. Clearly, that wasn't her perspective. She was late on edits again, months late, and didn't seem to care or make excuses or anything. I would work diligently to get everything done for her when I said I would, because anytime I'd fucked up deadlines in the past, no one had taken mercy on me. Plus I still had one final surgery to go through. A second round of liposuction around my tummy area so that it could fill up around the blobs of silicone and scar tissue that live now where my breasts used to be. It wasn't a necessary surgery, but it felt necessary for my mental health at the time. I thought if I just got my body looking a little bit better, Kyle would want to fuck me again. I wanted to have things done before then.

So, yeah, maybe I was harsh. But like Kyle, she seemed so desperate for an out.

Reflecting on all this, I leapt off the bed.

I had to read that conversation again. Because the common denominator has to be me, right? I opened my laptop and looked for our conversation. I had saved it to torture myself in one of my Google Docs, available to read offline.

"I'm a bit concerned that by the time we get this thing ready and out it will be close to November, and then editors will be starting to take holiday breaks," I'd expressed over Gchat.

"They will still be accepting submissions," she replied. "And I think because it's such a timely topic, they will read quickly—we've had pretty good responses so far."

This didn't match up with what she'd had told me in the past.

"I understand you are busy. I am as well. I also feel like I've been very patient and tried to turn things around as fast as possible and am always willing to do whatever I can to make things as painless as possible on your side. Please let me know if there's anything I can do more."

"You have been patient, and it's not your fault," she wrote. "My plan is to work on at least a chapter a day, so that we can send it out very soon."

Then I told her thanks, then we had a seemingly pleasant back and forth about what chapters needed editing. I said I liked the idea of changing the first four chapters into something more regional.

As I re-read this part of the Gchat, my heart began to race. I felt an urge to drink everything in the Airbnb and flee, abandon my dog even. Instead I held her close, dreading revisitation of my own visual.

Here it is, I thought, reading on, my palms starting to sweat.

"I hate to be in this situation where I even need to say this, and hope this doesn't make things awkward but I am honestly hurt about this. This is not how I like to work. Missing deadlines here and there, and I realize a lot of these are soft, is no big deal. But this is my career and I feel like this has become the norm as opposed to the exception. I know I may not be the most important author on your roster but I want to make sure you believe in my work as much as I do."

Hmm, okay, I was a bit harsh but not as bad as I remembered. My heart began to race a bit less. It was clear I'd been trying to avoid a fight.

Her reply: "Yes, these are all soft deadlines, and I can't help it if emergencies come up."

I remember at the time she said this, it pissed me off, because I was juggling so much, some of it cancer related, and never burdened her with it. Not once. When she offered help when I found out I had cancer, including a care package that never arrived, I just told her to work on my book. At first, she asked if I wanted to pause on writing, and part of me suspected she wanted me to. I said hell no, I need to write more than ever. Hell, despite having that dumb double mastectomy as I started grad school, I wasn't late on one homework assignment. I needed the work. I needed structure.

I needed writing more than ever.

I reflected, feeling tears well up with Amelia snuggling close.. Why couldn't she see that? She probably thought I was a snob, a bitch. I don't fucking know. Maybe it's entitled, I just need an outlet, something to love. Something bright.

*Okay read more, Gina.* I sat back up and read more of our messages. "I'm truly sorry that you are hurt by this. That was not my intention at all. Do you want to part ways? If you feel like we aren't communicating or on the same page, then that's a problem."

That's when I got a bit spicy: "If your response to 'I want to make sure you believe in my work as much as I do' is you asking if I want to part ways, that is a problem to me."

I was looking for validation. Ugh. I regret saying this. I was being insecure. I was getting so hurt because my feelings with her were merging with feelings of rejection from Kyle. And damn, I was being fucking impatient. Maybe because I'd lost patience in my relationship. They were all bleeding together, these feelings of unimportance, I suppose.

"I believe in this story," she replied. "I wouldn't if I didn't."

I remember noticing she said *story* and not my work, or me.

"I have surgery in a week and a half and all kinds of stuff I'm juggling, so if a soft deadline is missed, it's not just about my ego," I wrote. "I have to adjust my whole schedule."

"You're having surgery? For breast cancer again?"

"These are things I'm not going to burden you with because it's not your job. And I will always get what I need to done. It's just part of the reconstruction process. It's not a big deal. it's more like an annoyance."

"I didn't know this, and I do care, as an agent and a friend, I wish I had known, and I appreciate you telling me now," she said.

I didn't see her as a friend; I felt like there were clouds between us shielding our light from each other. These clouds seemed to be in front of all my friends lately. For the friends I loved the most, they were merely thin cirrus clouds, transparent. The more distant friends were covered up with cumulonimbus clouds, my favorite one from third grade.

"I really didn't see what the point would be." I remembered writing this with some arrogance. I didn't dare bring up the breakup with Kyle at this point. Didn't want to show more weakness or give her more outs or open holes for her to suggest I take time off, which I probably needed. "I thought we would have had it done by then. Lol trust me if I let you know of all the hurdles in my life nothing would ever get done. I'd prefer to deal with a lot of these things privately and like I said, I'm not trying to make things awkward but I feel like I need to let you know I was disappointed."

It wasn't so much that I was private in general. I was private because I didn't want her to push me to take time off work. What I wanted to tell her was that my perception of mortality has altered. I was worried about dying more than ever. I'd just completed the first run of cancer. Now I will be spending the rest of my remaining years alive waiting for the fatal round two. That's how it was for my parents and that's how it will, I assume, be for me.

Mom was 42 when she had cancer the first time, though in my memory sometimes I thought she was 40? Why? And she died by 50. And my dad, god why can't I remember?
Even though I was diagnosed at 32, the doctor told me I likely had it growing in me in my late twenties.. When is the second round going to be? 40?

I wanted to scream at her, "I HAVE TO GET AS MANY BOOKS OUT AS I CAN. LET ME HAVE THIS! I'M NOT GOING TO HAVE A NORMAL LIFE. LET ME AT LEAST HAVE THIS!"

I told her I had to go back to work but "thanks for taking the time to talk with me."

Her reply was "I'm glad you told me, and I appreciate you telling me what's going on and how this delay has affected you. Thanks for talking with me."

Alright, now that I was reading this a few months later, it wasn't *as* bad as I thought. I wasn't as bitchy or mean as I remembered. Was just trying to be clear and assert some boundaries, like with Otto. Assertive, forward, honest. It wasn't that bad. Certainly not as bad as I built it up to be. I was not bad as I built myself up to be.

I think what hurt the most was just knowing that expressing myself led to abandonment. I hate that feeling, that feeling which was just now as fresh as ever.

Then days later the abandonment email came from my agent. It didn't have a subject.

*Dear Gina,*

*I'm glad we talked last Monday. I've been thinking about our conversation, and it seems like we aren't working well together. You've said I hurt you when I wasn't able to stay on deadline. It's a sign that I'm not the best agent for you, and the book will have a better chance if we part ways now than if we went out on submission. I truly believe in the book, but sometimes that isn't enough. I'm deeply sorry that I hurt you, and I hope you find an agent that's a better fit. I wish you all the best in your publishing and creative endeavors.*

How I viewed it: Just another fucking person who is trying to teach me to submit to any treatment in the writing world or else I'm kicked the fuck out.

Tears ran down my cheeks as I focused on another crevice in the ceiling. I felt out. I felt like I had to submit to Otto's demands on how to respond to creepy guys or else I was out. And now I was out. Left on the side of the road for the vultures. The crevice on the ceiling began to look like the gash in my chest area.

What if I'm out forever? From love? From writing? I'm not the greatest writer and I know this. My words don't flow as eloquently or beautifully as others. That aspect doesn't come so naturally. But I can produce. I can just do it. That doesn't mean I can do it well. My attempts to find another agent had so far been unsuccessful. Even if I got one, which I fucking doubted, by the time they had me edit the thing and put it out on submission and it manages to get picked up maybe it will be published by the time I'm 40 and then I'll be dead. My attempts to find a partner have also been unsuccessful. Even if I do find someone, by the time we get to know each other, and get married, I'll be past 40 and too tired, too drained to want it as bad.

I jumped out of bed and ran to the fridge and, shaking, grabbed a cup from the countertop. The cup had a picture of Goofy on it, but he seemed off, like a bootleg Goofy. I filled him up with the rest of the wine. I became angry that I couldn't leave and find another corner store or something around me. It was too dark out there and I was scared. I sat on the patio and drank with rage, staring at the moonlit sky cascading shadows over the volcano.

How nice it would be if I had someone here with me. Someone like Otto but who understood women's issues more. A friend. But when Krystal was here, whose company I love, I still felt distant. I guess it would have to be someone I'm having sex with who was also cool. Ugh. Or better yet, Chinga.

I paced around the room and put some music on and put my headphones on so nobody could hear me listening to "7 Rooms of Gloom," the same song I heard on the airplane, though I doubt anyone could hear anything I did in the house. I felt so pathetic. Here I was in a beautiful foreign country and miserable.

I sat on the edge of the bed and rocked myself a bit. Calm down, Gina. I reminded myself, this is just part of the detox process. You're detoxing from what has been and likely will be the most serious relationship of your life. Let the gloom drip out here and not in Vermont where it will damage your life. Who cares if Otto bitches about you to Ted or other Siclians? Not like it will fuck up your life like when you fucked up your relationship with your agent.

"I saw Otto last night at Vucciria," Ted messaged me. I was on the train back to Palermo. He tacked on a winky face.

"Ya and? what did he say?"

"Nothing. We should hang soon."

"Yeah maybe," I said.

I saw a photo of the two together, taken by Ted. He had this smug smirk on his face. Did they think I was being passed around? Would they objectify me?

I refused to feel guilty about what I had done. Live like a guy, like a human, I reminded myself. I just fuck who I want to, at the moment at least, with no remorse.

"Maybe another sleepover when you come back?" he asked.

I told him, "I'd love to hang out, but I don't think I can sleep with anyone right now."

"No thanks, I don't want to be friendzoned," he replied.

"Okay. That's totally fine."

"So you want to hang with some sex?"

"No."

Ugh, is this a bad translation, a cultural thing or is he just being a jerk? Or tidbits of all?

The days continued. My Palermo apartment was starting to feel like a windowless cave made of cheap European plastic caving in on me.

The sole window in the apartment, a slit of a window really, only looked out to the hallways. A sliver of light would sometimes cast down from the open sky in the afternoon, but it felt like it was always so dark on the outside, even when I wasn't sure what time it was. I could check the clock, but I'd often just close the narrow window with its interior wooden shutters and lie in bed surrounded by walls and the kitchen before me. It reminded me of the times I lived in studios. For a few years in Montreal, ages 18-20, I could see the kitchen from my bed in a studio tinier than a dorm room. When I moved back to Vermont, I could see the toilet through the slightly open bathroom door, just feet away from my squat mini-fridge.

After me and Otto's non-breakup breakup, I began replacing sex with food. I gave up on trying to sleep with guys in Palermo. I just didn't have the energy anymore. Instead, I began to focus on the grocery store below me. I'd make pasta with all local ingredients, then eat a serving size for two and wait around for hours until I could eat again, to the point where I felt like a Sarde a Beccafico myself, stuffed.

I'd lie in bed feeling full, thinking about what I should cook. *Maybe cut up the half pumpkin in the fridge and use that as the meat part of my dinner, then make pasta. You can home make the sauce with all the herbs you got.*

The mattress vibrated. I looked at the phone. Chinga was calling. I suddenly jolted into alertness and literally fanned my face with my hand for a second before answering.

"Hello?" I asked in a joking, nasally nerd voice that Chinga and I often intoned when living together, traveling together, hanging out together.

"What's up," he said in a detached voice, like it was a sentence and not a question.

"Oh, you know." I was smiling and my heart was beating fast as my mind darted around for the right thing to say, for *a* thing to say.

"How's Italy?"

I could tell by the affectation of his voice that he was drunk.

"It's pretty good. Still trying to figure out what to do with my life."

"Yeah?"

"Yeah," I said. Before I could ask what he was up to he said, "You know Gina, you're awesome. You've always been awesome. If, ya know, you ever need a place to stay, you can come here for a bit maybe. You could stay here. I have a desk you could work at."

"Chinga," I hesitated to ask if he was drunk. "Thank you, that's very generous of you! And yeah, I'd love to come visit."

"You can even use my Jeep. Actually, let me call you right back. I'm getting some pizza delivered."

"Domino's?"

"Yup. Call ya right back."

"Okay, bye!"

I put the phone down and wandered to my current mini-fridge. I peered inside and grabbed a tub of leftover pasta. I took a fork from the drying rack and poked at some of the cold noodles drenched in red sludge. I took a bite.

The phone rang again. Chinga was chewing too.

"How's the pizza? Was it the same juggalo girl who delivered when we lived together?"

"No," he answered as if it were a serious question.

Soon, the conversation turned to dating.

"Yeah, so, I mean, Germans, amiright?"

"I did Nazi this coming," he joked.

"He asked if I was going to write about him, like a poem about him. I told him if I did, he probably wouldn't be happy about it."

Chinga laughed.

"Maybe I *should* write him a poem," I said.

"How poetic," he said.

"He's not used to me writing about him, not like you," I joked.

"Well, I hope you don't write about killing him."

"No, only very few can reach that level of specialness in my heart." *Uh oh, I hope he doesn't get awkward about this.*

Chinga laughed, "Oh yeah," as if he was just remembering for the first time in a long time. "Well I guess I should do some painting and go to bed but ya, you should come visit. Would be good to see ya."

"Yeah, I'd love that. I definitely will. Good chatting."

"You too."

## 8

I tried to remind myself how lucky I am.

I thought back to when I was out for dinner with a friend in Brooklyn.

"You have so many guys that love you," she told me.

"What?" I took a swig of wine.

"Yeah, I was talking to my sister about that the other day. At the fashion show there were so many dudes around you."

"Yeah, but those were my friends. I don't think I slept with any of them."

"You got a lot of dudes that love you."

Well yes, and also the friends I sleep with.

I thought of my former friend with benefits, Jon, whom I slept with for four or five years. We'd typically have sex once a month or so and would halt it if one of us was in a relationship. There was never any drama and I never worried about what he was doing or who he was sleeping with. Still, I liked him a lot. I often wondered how I could turn it into a relationship. Once, on *his* birthday, he took *me* out for dinner. Still, I just couldn't find the words or ways to make him my boyfriend. Maybe he didn't want that.

I thought about my other friend Brett, who I slept with on and off for years. We'd go to art shows or bars. One time we had sex in a bar bathroom. I thought of it as dating, I think. Did he? Or was I just a friend he touched sometimes? Who knows? We never communicated about it.

I turned on the blue lamp next to me so I wouldn't be just sitting in the darkness. The blue cast a gloomy shade on the white of Amelia's fur.

"Amelia! What am I doing here?" I said in a baby voice. "Did I stay here an extra month for a boy? The hope of a comfortable future, the kind of future I am taught to want?"

I flipped her long-haired ear over gently and rubbed her neck.

"Why can't I just be a pampered dog?"

She wagged her tail slightly.

There were only 22 days to go. I knew my time was rapidly diminishing and I'd have to pack up my stuff and go on back. I thought by now I would have figured out where I wanted to be, but was more confused than ever.

Maybe I'll move back to New York? Maybe. I didn't want to make the decision. Any big life decision. I didn't want to have to start over again. I just wanted to be comfortable, to have finally moved into a permanent home, the final destination. It felt like I'd been so close to that. My whole life I'd been chasing it and now had failed and there was no way I could ever get it in time.

Kyle and I may have not been fucking, but one of our favorite pastimes was to look at houses. So, my sex life isn't great, I told myself, but I was comfortable. Sure, I was lonely but it was stable. We could get a house and then all my stuff would be in there and I wouldn't have to worry about packing or moving or figuring out what to do next. I would have already achieved it and isn't that the dream? At the end of the day though, I knew that wasn't right.

Now, it pained me to even think about packing my clothing to get on an airplane, let alone move to another state or city and into what I assumed would be another temporary living situation before making further decisions which would require further packing and further moving, decisions I just didn't want to make anymore. The thought of it all was so draining that I literally had to sit down to even attempt to process it all.

Now, more than two months in, I was starting to get to know the people at the Cavu language exchange fairly well. Well, most aspects about them. I knew that the Lithuanian couple loved to travel. They had two cats with them, long, elegant, and patterned like leopards. I knew Marco was obsessed with cinema and wasn't into chasing girls. I think he liked girls but was here to make platonic friends. Vincenzo was often goofy, amicable, always smiling. Sometimes he'd put his arms around me and tell me to look up at the moon, calling it romantic. Then there was Frank, who looked like a baby version of my Uncle Frank, who was from Sicily and married my aunt, his first cousin, in an arranged marriage in the 1940s. Frank, like Ted, was into Eastern European women and still had a Couchsurfing account, mainly for this purpose.

I barely knew what people did for work. Despite hanging out every week for months, the topic never came up. One mid-February night when my departure was inching forward, it finally did.

"I'm a doctor after all," Vincenzo told me.

"Oh wow, you don't seem like a doctor."

"What does that mean?" he asked, smiling.

"You're chill. You don't think you're better than everyone else."

"Well, duh. It's not my identity. It's just my job."

I sighed.

Being a writer *was* my identity.

Suddenly I felt like I was indeed in the movie *Eat, Pray, Love,* a scene in which Gilbert is sitting at a table in Italy with international folks. One asked Gilbert who she was, what word she felt represented her best. She thought for a while before settling on "writer."

"Yeah, but that's what you do," one of the people at the table said.

"That isn't who you are, no?" asked another.

"Maybe you're a woman in search of her word," her friend suggested.

Ugh, I rolled my eyes. That's happening to me now. I guess I'm not so different from this live laugh love bitch as I thought. She's just had it a bit easier than me in life, I assume, and is a bit luckier but really, at our heart, we are both Americans who identify with our work and feel alone. For Christ's sake, I even have the word 'write' tattooed on my arm. It's inked on me, that's how married I am to it as my identity.

I woke up around nine a.m. and got Amelia suited up. Even though it was about 50 degrees, a woman came up to me shrieking about how she should be wearing a coat.

I walked by the water. The waves were especially rough that day. They were splashing up the rocks. Every 40 seconds or so, a big wave would actually make it onto the sidewalk. I became fixed on that point and began drifting into thoughts. Today I had to—

Ow. Both my knees smashed against the pavement below. It hurt but I didn't want to express pain. Instead, I channeled the ache radiating through my legs and entire body on trying to get back up, on trying to not make a scene. I looked around. Nobody seemed to have noticed. I looked behind and saw a crack in the sidewalk.

I struggled to get up and, damn, my knees still hurt.

Ugh, there were holes in my favorite black jeans. I could see red coming out of the holes.

I looked in one. Not too bad. The right knee though? Looked like there was a flap of skin.

*Oh goddamn it.* My inner self curled up like a pill bug. I felt queasy as I put my finger into the hole to make sure I couldn't see muscle or bone. The whole wasn't big enough to see everything. Time to walk home. Walking wasn't bad. When I got home, I took the pants off, carefully unpeeling the parts stuck to the bloodied knees. My left knee just had a bad scrape, but there was definitely a flap of skin hanging off the right one.

I messaged Vincnezo over Whatsapp.

"I am an idiot and fell. I think I need stitches but I'm not sure."

"Oh no! Send picture."

I did.

"Yes, you need stitches," he wrote back.

"Thank you. I was afraid of that. I don't have insurance. Is there any place I can go to where it will be less expensive? Where should I go? I don't have insurance."

"No! It's free anywhere! We are not in America! Closest emergency room."

The ER closest to me, according to Google maps, was a mile and a half away in an "even more run down" area than where I lived, an unknown neighborhood Otto once pointed out to me, more to the left of the train station, deeper into it all. Toward the sounds of the deepest explosions at night.

Ugh. Now I really needed, wanted, no—needed, Uber access.

I looked at the time. 11:58 am. By the time I got there and had it looked at, if I was extremely lucky, I would be well into my work day. *Fuck it, I'll work from the emergency room.* I scooped my laptop off the table and crammed it into my tiny leather backpack.

I walked and walked, past cafes offering the same treats in slightly different styles and lights. Brown and tan street dogs sat stoically on the sidewalk as people walked past.

Soon I was sitting in an emergency room, writing articles about women murdered by their boyfriends after they rejected them. Blood dripped down my leg. I started a new article, about former high school teacher Tad Cummins, who kidnapped his own student and ran away with her.

*A Tennessee teacher who was on the run for weeks with a 15-year-old student was sentenced Wednesday to 20 years in prison.*
My knee was still oozing. I'd been there over two hours, so I went to the front desk and asked if I could get an alcohol swab to clean it myself as I waited.

"Let me see." She looked at the hole in my jeans. "Oh."

Within five minutes, I was in a room with a doctor who chatting about his brother in New York.

"I like Brooklyn," he said while weaving black thread through my skin, "but the food isn't as good."

That night, I shared my little snafu at Cavu with a few expats.

"How did you get to the hospital?"

I walked," I said quietly.

"What are you, an idiot?" the American woman yelled. "Why didn't you call an ambulance?"

"I don't know. That idea seems dramatic. Plus I've always been told that if you don't need-need an ambulance, better to just drive yourself or whatever. Too expensive."

"Hello?! Not here! Free healthcare. Earth to Gina."

"Ya know," Vincenzo said. "You could have called a taxi."

"What?" I said. "I thought there weren't any."

"Oh there is, here, I'll get you the name of the app."

"You mean there was a fucking taxi app here all along? I think I need another drink."

# Nicole

It had been over a month and a half since my brother left, aka over a month and a half of being unable to fully connect with someone in person, someone I really knew-knew who could understand my ticks.

Standing in the lobby of the airport waiting for my cousin, I looked around the room and remembered the movie *Love, Actually* and how much I hated it, mostly because nothing like the relationships in that movie had ever *actually* happened to me.

Nicole came out wearing a skirt and thigh high socks with sparkling Gucci shoes, very fashionable in the way I like, the way Otto described the umbrella. Her style and blonde hair stuck out amongst the monotone hair and the classical black pants and jackets around her. I stood there a muted version of myself, wearing black jeans, a black top, and a black scarf, melding into the crowd with my black mop. As soon as she came bouncing toward me like a gemstone, I felt comfort and relief. I could shine now too. At least for a few days, I could lean more toward my shiny self and not dull myself up out of fear of the dark. We could walk Amelia together at night and if we got stranded on the road, we wouldn't be as alone, as vulnerable.

"Hi!"

"Ahhhhh, so good to see you!"

She'd rented a car for a road trip together around the island during her visit. We arrived at the parking lot and realized they had given her a Jeep.

"Oh my god," I said as we approached the vehicle. "I haven't seen a car this big since November. It's all teeny cars and vespas here."

"Oh no," Nicole laughed, "maybe they thought as an American I'd want this car."

The deal was that she'd rented it and I'd drive it. She was a little more trepidatious of a driver than me.

"I'm more like Grandma," she joked. "I like being driven around."

Our Grandma never got her driver's license. She married our grandfather young, which was obviously very typical at the time, and just never got around to it. I had a few female friends in similar boats now. Friends who haven't driven in years because their husbands or boyfriends primarily drive. I wondered how much my life would slow down if I didn't drive.

"We'll just do what Google Maps tells us to do," I said.

We planned to visit Prizzi, the town our grandmother's mother fled as a child. The road to our heritage was not an easy one.

It led us onto roads that grew narrower, rockier, and filled with potholes. At one point we passed a small ravine, nothing too threatening, but the guardrail alongside it was so mangled it looked like it had been curled, like the bridge in *Evil Dead* but to a much less dramatic and cartoonish extreme.

We wound up hills, the white road became even slimmer.

"Dude is this becoming a one-way street?" I asked.

"Yikes," Nicole said holding Amelia in her lap, looking at the map on her phone. "I mean, it does say we are on the right track."

While the road was bumpy and potholed, it was generally smooth, which I only realized once it transformed into gravel. Suddenly I driving on millions of pebbles, crunchy and slippery all at once.

Up, up, and up, the hills around us looking more and more pointy. Then we were on the tippy top of one.

"Oh god," I sat looking down one of the steepest hills I've ever been on, minus perhaps a roller coaster. "Is this a road for cars?'

There was nowhere but down. I could see Nicole panicking, holding Amelia tightly as I told her, "I got this."

But did I?

The tires of the Jeep began slipping as I slowly tried to make it downhill. My foot was on the brakes, tapping them gently as I struggled to steer, pebbles flicking from under the tires, making sounds like inverted raindrops beneath the car. A large hole appeared in front of us, like a pothole but wider, and at the bottom of the kind of angle that only belongs in geometry class.

"Fuck," I said as the car hit it and made a thump, then a clunk from under the car.

We were over the worst part, as far as we could tell.

"Jesus Christ." I turned to my cousin. "Thought we were gonna have to get rescued with a helicopter."

I stopped the car and put it in park. I got out and looked under for damage but there was nothing visible.

"We should make sure we are on a road for cars. This looks like a road for a tractor."

"I know," she said. "Good thing we got a Jeep. How does anyone drive on this?"

"Can't imagine what would have happened if we were in a tiny Italian car."

"Yeah, this is the road. This is what Google maps is telling us."

"Well, fuck."

After driving through hills and desolate roads, passing plenty of signs reading "watch out for falling rocks," then passing said falling rocks, we finally saw our heritage hill on the horizon. While the slopes around it were green and buildingless, the mound Prizzi was built on looked like a lego set. There were so many buildings tightly packed toward the tip of the mountain. Layers and layers of clay shingles. We pulled over to stand and gawk at the town with all its winding roads zipping between ancient homes.

We drove onward and spent the night in the city of Ragusa, a town as dense as Palermo but emptier than my hometown at 3 am on a Tuesday night. When we woke up, we wandered the streets looking for a cafe, or anything open really.

"I can start to understand why all the locals were so against me living in Bagheria. Small towns here really have nothing going on."

"Like *nothing.*"

"Literally nothing, how do people here get their food?"

"I guess you have to know where the open shops are. Maybe everyone does most things at home."

Right then and there, a miniature green pickup truck overflowing with vegetables, green leaves, and boxes of fruits barreled down the road, the driver yelling through a megaphone. A woman in a house yelled something Italian from her window. He stopped. The lady vanished briefly as the driver gathered a handful of oranges and some bananas from the front seat. She handed him some coins through the window and got fruits and veggies in exchange.

We visited the town of Taormina and checked out Teatro Antico, the ruins of an ancient Greek theater. Standing in the rubble, we could see Mount Etna smoking in the distance. We decided to drive as close to the volcano as we could before it got dark. We drove for hours toward the billowing smoke, but as we began our ascent up a hill that seemed quite close to the smoking crater, the roads started to grow narrower and the yellow sun began blushing pink.

"How does our near future in roading look on Google Maps?" I asked.

"Hard to tell."

Scared of repeating our previous expedition, especially in the dark, we decided to turn back.

On the way back to Palermo, we shared details of past relationships and talked about the people we'd loved and lost.

"I think I realized my friends with benefits relationships were the healthiest and most fulfilling in my life," I said. "I've had many and several have lasted years if not over a decade. Actually, calling them friends with benefits reduces the value of these relationships. Lovers would be more apt I guess."

"Yeah I get that," Nicole said. "I guess we take after Uncle Peter in the sense that we are more the free spirits in the family. Traditional relationships just aren't our thing."

"Yeah. I mean, I wish they were, at least for me."

I glanced up at the Big Dipper on the horizon as I drove on a highway where ours were the only pair of headlights.

# Epilogue

"Buono," I said, as I rolled a soft mint green suitcase with pink trimming through a store and placed it onto the counter.

56 Euro. It was just big enough to cram all the clothing and junk I'd accumulated over the past three months. Just a few days away from flying back.

I could almost hear Otto's voice saying, "What a fucking American thing to do," and it was.

As I rolled it down the street, I angrily told myself, *that's what I am, I guess.* I suddenly had the urge to go to a Starbucks. I wanted iced coffee or an iced matcha green tea latte. Give me something iced and sugary. For my fat, capitalist brain. I wanted to be wearing sweatpants and dressing like a slob.

After forty minutes of rolling it over stones and cracks in the sidewalks, I brought my new suitcase into my temporary home, just hours away from abandoning it so someone else could fill it up. I unzipped the suitcase and placed it on my bedroom floor. Amelia peered inside it with worry. She knows what suitcases mean. I went to the flimsy closet and began taking clothes off their plastic hooks. Velvet blazer, velvet shorts, a tank top I bought on a whim on the way to see my Italian tutor. My new leather shoes. I stuffed them all in.

Amelia began to whine.

"Don't worry. We're not leaving. Yet. And you're coming with me."

She knows what 'you're coming with me' means.

"Want to go for a walk?"

She barked and stomped around, tail wagging. I attached her leash to her harness and walked her out. I took her through the dark little tunnel with the religious statue in it. Two people were there, clearly having sex. A man had a woman wearing thigh highs up against the wall and they were breathing hard.

I walked faster. Amelia tried to eat a cannolo crumble on the ground. I pulled her forward.

"Come on," I whispered.

We got back in and I sat at the table, the window to the hallway allowing darkness to creep into the room. I sat there and thought back to when the crack of the window was full of mid-morning light. It was 11 am or so, I knew my time to start work was approaching, and me and Otto had just finished eating some pastries he'd brought over. They were puffy and light and flaky and got crumbs all over the table.

Then we spooned on the couch, his arms around me as a slight breeze from the window hit my face. It transported me once again to the hope of happiness.

"Hold on a sec," I said, closing the window. "Maybe I'm not meant for romantic happiness." I climbed back on the couch and he put his arm around me.

"What the hell are you talking about?"

"Nevermind. I'm just being emotional. I'm really enjoying the warmth of your body right now. Just wish I could ziplock a cuddle session and live inside it for the rest of my life."

"You're silly." He kissed my forehead.

I thought back to something a very brash medium told me. He brought me into a secluded room set up for him at an art event, his face expressing disgust as we passed by a loud, obnoxious man.

After he shut the door, he said, "He has a bleak future."

He said something about that man's soul being bad, I forget the exact words.

The lights were off, there were some candles.

He said that there were a lot of deceased people trying to talk to me and most, according to his translation, had messages about or for other people.

"There's another person that was in the same accident as her, it seems, who is trying to talk to you. A guy with beautiful blue eyes wants you to give a message to someone who has lots of tattoos. Your friend. He wants you to tell her that he's with her, watching her. That she should never feel lonely. That he loves her."

My mother was also trying to speak to me, according to the medium.

But she didn't have anything loving to say.

"Your mom, she said you have to stop living like a kid. You have to take more responsibility for your finances."

I smiled because that is likely what she would say. I haven't heard that typical kind of mom-nagging since a few months after I turned 20. It was nice, but empty too.

"Your mom, well it's kind of weird for a mom, she doesn't come around to watch you very much. Your grandma does but that's only because you look like your mom."

I flinched. Everyone tells me how much I look like her and talk like her.

"She, your mom, does want me to tell you that she does look at you from your desk in your room," the psychic said. "I don't know what that means."

He then told me that my financial situation would get bad, real bad, and then soon become very good and that I would be very successful. But, he said, in the love and support department, not so much.

"Yeah, nobody is really gonna give you what you need," he said. "You are..,"

He paused for a moment seemingly pondering if I was worthy of love.

"Yes. You do deserve..." He sighed. "You are a very good person, you have a very good heart. You do deserve love."

Not knowing what to do or say, I said thanks.

"Alright, I'm going to need a drink and a cigarette after this reading," he said.

My god, I thought. Are my aura and future that disturbing? Does he know something about my future that is terrible like what he knows about the obnoxious man? I was feeling all kinds of feelings, most of which contained elements of sadness and rejection. Why wouldn't my own mother want to watch over me? Why were the only words of encouragement and love said to me by a dead classmate who wanted me to pass them on to someone else?

I wanted to write it off as insane because I didn't want to have a lonely life. I pointed to the desk thing as a mistake. That didn't make sense. Yes, I did have a desk in my room and yes not every bedroom has a desk in it, but whatever. Then I got home, and low and behold, on my desk, alongside many other trinkets, was a picture of me, her, and my dad in the ball pit at Sesame Place.

Yikes. Now everything the medium said felt so much more real. So much more terrifying. Was he right? How does this work? Is there fate? I felt like I was in Philosophy 101 again. Can I change the future or is it just stuck like that? If you just allow what you expect is destined for you to passively happen, then there's likely no other option.

I remember thinking I'd proved the medium wrong when I met Kyle, when he told me he wanted to marry me one beautiful afternoon. I can still recall exactly where I was standing. In our dining room atop my parents' old rug. They treasured that rug. Now it was full of stains from lugging it through my chaotic life. He said it with one foot on the rug, and the other on the kitchen linoleum.

I remember returning to thinking the medium was indeed right when our relationship crumbled. I felt like no matter how hard I tried, guys who are obsessed with me for months would eventually just become obsessed with my flaws.

I thought back to the end of *Eat, Pray, Love*. She took a chance on love again even though she was scared, even though she didn't feel balanced, and she got it. Someone took a chance on her.

I guess I'll just keep fucking people and maybe one of them will take that mutual chance with me. I'll just keep writing about murder so I'll have money to eat, so I can stay alive, so I can keep fucking people until I find a healthy love.

Big thank you to the following friends, who provided immense professional and/or emotional support during the writing and/or publishing of this book:

Chrystin Ondersma
Kim Vodicka
Kim Göransson
Hillary Leftwich
Freddy La Force
Suzi Boeglin
Laura Feiner
Bradford Masoni

**Gina Tron** is the author of several books, including her debut memoir *You're Fine*, which *Interview Magazine* called "vibrant, darkly funny, and courageously candid" in 2014. Her 2020 poetry book *Star 67* contains a poem that has been nominated for a Pushcart Prize.

*Employment*, her second book of poetry, touches "on the dark side of many of the jobs she has held; of sexism and corruption, sexual harassment, boredom, and plain old poor management," according to the *New York Post*.

She wrote as a true crime reporter for *Oxygen* for six years and wrote reported pieces for various outlets, including *The Washington Post, VICE, Politico,* and *The Daily Beast*. She is an adjunct professor at Norwich University in Vermont, and edits copy about substance use disorder and mental health. She holds an MFA from Vermont College of Fine Arts, but more importantly, she holds a lot of eggs and pasta as she mopes about town.